Medieval Philosophy: A Very Short Introduction

VERY SHORT INTRODUCTIONS are for anyone wanting a stimulating and accessible way into a new subject. They are written by experts, and have been translated into more than 40 different languages.

The Series began in 1995, and now covers a wide variety of topics in every discipline. The VSI library now contains over 450 volumes—a Very Short Introduction to everything from Psychology and Philosophy of Science to American History and Relativity—and continues to grow in every subject area.

Very Short Introductions available now:

ACCOUNTING Christopher Nobes
ADVERTISING Winston Fletcher
AFRICAN AMERICAN RELIGION
    Eddie S. Glaude Jr
AFRICAN HISTORY John Parker and
    Richard Rathbone
AFRICAN RELIGIONS Jacob K. Olupona
AGNOSTICISM Robin Le Poidevin
ALEXANDER THE GREAT Hugh Bowden
ALGEBRA Peter M. Higgins
AMERICAN HISTORY Paul S. Boyer
AMERICAN IMMIGRATION
    David A. Gerber
AMERICAN LEGAL HISTORY
    G. Edward White
AMERICAN POLITICAL HISTORY
    Donald Critchlow
AMERICAN POLITICAL PARTIES
    AND ELECTIONS L. Sandy Maisel
AMERICAN POLITICS Richard M. Valelly
THE AMERICAN PRESIDENCY
    Charles O. Jones
THE AMERICAN
    REVOLUTION Robert J. Allison
AMERICAN SLAVERY
    Heather Andrea Williams
THE AMERICAN WEST Stephen Aron
AMERICAN WOMEN'S HISTORY
    Susan Ware
ANAESTHESIA Aidan O'Donnell
ANARCHISM Colin Ward
ANCIENT ASSYRIA Karen Radner
ANCIENT EGYPT Ian Shaw
ANCIENT EGYPTIAN ART AND
    ARCHITECTURE Christina Riggs

ANCIENT GREECE Paul Cartledge
THE ANCIENT NEAR EAST
    Amanda H. Podany
ANCIENT PHILOSOPHY Julia Annas
ANCIENT WARFARE Harry Sidebottom
ANGELS David Albert Jones
ANGLICANISM Mark Chapman
THE ANGLO - SAXON AGE John Blair
THE ANIMAL KINGDOM
    Peter Holland
ANIMAL RIGHTS David DeGrazia
THE ANTARCTIC Klaus Dodds
ANTISEMITISM Steven Beller
ANXIETY Daniel Freeman and
    Jason Freeman
THE APOCRYPHAL GOSPELS
    Paul Foster
ARCHAEOLOGY Paul Bahn
ARCHITECTURE Andrew Ballantyne
ARISTOCRACY William Doyle
ARISTOTLE Jonathan Barnes
ART HISTORY Dana Arnold
ART THEORY Cynthia Freeland
ASTROBIOLOGY David C. Catling
ATHEISM Julian Baggini
AUGUSTINE Henry Chadwick
AUSTRALIA Kenneth Morgan
AUTISM Uta Frith
THE AVANT GARDE David Cottington
THE AZTECS David Carrasco
BACTERIA Sebastian G. B. Amyes
BARTHES Jonathan Culler
THE BEATS David Sterritt
BEAUTY Roger Scruton
BESTSELLERS John Sutherland

For more information visit our website:

John Marenbon

MEDIEVAL PHILOSOPHY

A Very Short Introduction

OXFORD
UNIVERSITY PRESS

OXFORD
UNIVERSITY PRESS

Great Clarendon Street, Oxford, OX2 6DP,
United Kingdom

Oxford University Press is a department of the University of Oxford.
It furthers the University's objective of excellence in research, scholarship,
and education by publishing worldwide. Oxford is a registered trade mark of
Oxford University Press in the UK and in certain other countries

© John Marenbon 2016

The moral rights of the author have been asserted

First edition published in 2016

Impression: 7

Published in the United States of America by Oxford University Press
198 Madison Avenue, New York, NY 10016, United States of America

British Library Cataloguing in Publication Data
Data available

Library of Congress Control Number: 2015947580

ISBN 978-0-19-966322-4

Printed in Great Britain by
Ashford Colour Press Ltd., Gosport, Hampshire.

Contents

Medieval Philosophy

Acknowledgements

I am enormously grateful to Sheila Lawlor, Maximus Marenbon, and Tony Street for their comments on drafts of this book which saved me from unclarity, confusion, and error. Peter Adamson went carefully through the whole manuscript as the publisher's (originally anonymous) reader, correcting errors and making many valuable suggestions for improvement, which I have followed. I am also most grateful to Dan Harding for his thorough and intelligent copy-editing, to Saraswathi Ethiraju for managing the production of the book and to Jenny Nugee who has seen me through the various stages of the project with an ideal mixture of efficiency, charm and patience.

List of illustrations

Chapter 1
Introduction

A famous fresco sums up the popular image today of philosophy in the Middle Ages. In the centre of *The Triumph of St Thomas Aquinas* by Benozzo Gozzoli, sits Aquinas, holding open a copy of one of his *summas*, his face fixed and impassive. On either side, behind him and subservient, stand Plato and Aristotle. Trampled beneath his feet is the Arabic philosopher, Averroes, while in the bottom tier of the picture, the Pope sits in Council, proclaiming Aquinas as 'the light of the Church'. The upper tier is occupied by the Evangelists and, at the top, God himself, who is saying 'Thomas, you have spoken well about me' (see Figure 1).

In the popular image—which is shared by many medievalists and most professional philosophers—'Aquinas' is almost a synonym for medieval philosophy, which it locates in Western Europe, and principally in his lifetime and the fifty or so years before and after, from the early 13th to the mid-14th century. Medieval philosophy is seen as a type of Church teaching, a monolithic doctrine in which there is no room for debate except about details; where ancient philosophy plays its part, but is subordinated in a Christian synthesis, and Arabic (and Jewish) thinkers are there to be used and trampled upon in triumph: hardly philosophy at all. It might fascinate some people, but this approach makes it at best a sideline, which a thinking person, or even a philosopher, can happily ignore.

1. Benozzo Gozzoli, *The Triumph of St Thomas Aquinas*.

This image is wrong on every point. The aim of this book is to put a truer image in its place. Having a false image of medieval philosophy not only obscures a fascinating area of intellectual enquiry but also, as will be argued in Chapter 10, distorts our whole understanding of philosophy and its history.

Three mistakes about medieval philosophy

The first error in the popular image is geographical. Medieval philosophy was practised over an area of roughly ten million square miles, stretching from the west of Ireland to Uzbekistan, from Gothenburg to the Gulf of Aden. The point is not simply that there were philosophers in these places; so there were, in the same period, even further afield, in India, China, and elsewhere. It is, rather, that the philosophy done in this vast region belonged to a single group of intertwined traditions, all going back to ancient Greece: Western philosophy, but in a way which makes us rethink what we mean by 'Western'.

Although the deep roots of medieval philosophy go back to Plato and Aristotle, the trunk from which the four main branches developed was the thinking of the late ancient schools of Athens and Alexandria, from which each of the traditions inherited a largely similar body of texts. These four branches are: Latin Christian philosophy, as practised throughout Western Europe; Greek Christian philosophy, as developed in the Byzantine Empire; Arabic philosophy; and Jewish philosophy. These four traditions do not merely share a common origin—like the intertwining branches of a tree, they are linked in their development through translations: from Greek into Arabic and Latin; Arabic into Latin and Hebrew; and Latin into Greek and Hebrew.

The interconnections are evident even in the nomenclature. 'Arabic philosophy' is used here (not 'Islamic philosophy') so as to emphasize that Jews and Christians, as well as Muslims,

philosophized in Arabic, often as intellectual colleagues or adversaries. Yet Jewish philosophy—including that written in Arabic—is distinguished as a separate tradition, because of the way in which Jewish philosophy in Hebrew links back to Jewish philosophy in Arabic. Chapter 2 will provide an outline map of the four traditions, showing how they connect to the ancient schools and sources and with each other.

The second mistake in the popular image is about chronology. Where and when the period in the history of philosophy labelled 'medieval' begins and ends is, of course, a matter of custom and choice—and there are good reasons, looking at the continuity of the traditions, for thinking of it as stretching from about AD 200 until the middle or end of the 17th century (and later still in Islam). Whether these wide limits, or the more restricted usual ones—roughly 500 (or sometimes later) to 1500—are taken, there is no good reason for giving special prominence to the years from 1250 to 1350. Even in the Latin tradition alone, the two centuries before 1250 and the three after 1350 are no less rich, and once the other traditions are considered, it becomes clear that none of the medieval centuries was without interesting philosophy.

The third error in the popular conception is about the relationship between medieval philosophy and religion. Part of the error has already been explained: the relationship in question is not just between philosophy and Latin Christianity, but also between philosophy and Judaism, Islam, Greek Christianity, and indeed the monotheistic religion developed by the late ancient pagan Greek philosophers themselves in reaction to Christianity. However, this explanation does nothing to answer the accusation underlying the popular image: that medieval philosophical thinking is so intertwined with religion and subservient to it that it is not really philosophy at all.

One way of replying would be to accept the terms of the accusation but say that is unjustified. Despite the religious

reference of three of them, the names for the different traditions designate cultural areas, and in each of them much philosophical work was done which either, like logic, had nothing obviously to do with religion, or else was deliberately kept apart from it. But this reply is not completely satisfactory. Medieval cultural traditions were intimately tied to religious ones (though not always to a single religious tradition: witness the cases of Jewish and Christian Arabic philosophers). Much of the finest philosophy was done by theologians in the course of tackling specifically theological problems. And, even when philosophers of the time intentionally isolated their thinking from their faith, in order to justify themselves they had to take up a position about reason and its relationship to revelation.

Medieval philosophy and historical analysis

A proper answer to the charge that medieval philosophy is religion or theology in disguise needs to recognize that the accusation contains, in distorted form, an important element of truth. To sort out the truth from the falsehood, we need to look more carefully at what is involved in writing the history of philosophy.

The accusation is based on the assumption that there is a block of material identifiable as medieval philosophy which is then found insufficiently philosophical. But in fact the word 'philosophy', used in connection with the Middle Ages (or indeed any period before the mid-18th century), is anachronistic. Whatever the current debates about the philosophy of philosophy, we all have a rough and ready, practical grasp of what sort of books will be in the philosophy section of a library or what a student is likely to study for a philosophy degree. In the Middle Ages, there was no such subject. Although many questions were discussed that are similar to those which philosophers debate today, and with similar methods of analysis and argument, these enquiries were not grouped into a single discipline. They were intermixed, not just with theology but also with what we would now consider

branches of natural science, such as biology, psychology, physics, astronomy, and with mathematics, music, grammar, and rhetoric.

A good way to write the history of medieval (or ancient, or early modern) philosophy, then, is to start from what we now recognize and find important as philosophical questions and look for them in texts from the past, using 'philosophy' in its contemporary sense to make our initial selection from the medieval material. By doing so, we can be sure that what we produce will count uncontentiously as what we understand now as a history of *philosophy*.

On this approach, which I call 'historical analysis', the extent to which medieval philosophical material is entangled with, or even in some cases subordinated to, theological and other discussions is no longer an objection. The question is simply whether, from our contemporary starting point, we find among the heterogeneous material interesting treatments of what we recognize as important philosophical questions—and here the answer, as even this short book will show, is resoundingly positive.

Such an avowedly anachronistic approach to the history of medieval philosophy might seem to save the philosophy at the cost of sacrificing the history. But historical analysis has two stages. After posing their questions and selecting their material from a contemporary perspective, the investigators must overcome this necessary anachronism by placing the philosophical discussions they have isolated back within their intellectual context—which, for the Middle Ages, is above all a religious one. This is the element of truth in the mistaken image of medieval philosophy as theology in disguise.

This book takes historical analysis as its approach. Historical analysis requires much more space to present each argument than most intellectual historians are used to allowing. There will be space to look at just four problems which were debated

throughout the Middle Ages, and which still, if in somewhat different forms, excite philosophers today. In each case, the focus will be on two contrasting medieval philosophers, one from the Latin tradition and one from the Arabic or Jewish tradition, but the discussions will range over other thinkers too. Before these problems are considered, the first half of the book (Chapters 2–5) sets them within their context, providing a general introduction to the whole field and giving an idea of the range of questions discussed by medieval philosophers.

Chapter 2
A map of earlier medieval philosophy

Late antiquity and its Platonic schools

Broadly speaking, medieval philosophy in its different traditions had its origins in the philosophy of ancient Greece, principally the thinking of Aristotle and Plato, as understood and elaborated in late antiquity (*c.* AD 200–500), especially in the Platonic schools.

From the time of Plotinus (d. 270) onwards, a revived Platonism drove the philosophical schools which had been popular for the preceding five centuries (Epicureanism, Scepticism, and, especially, Stoicism) into obscurity. Plotinus claimed just to be interpreting Plato, but he went far further in mapping out of the intelligible world: the realm of true being which is grasped, not through our senses, but by thought. Plato had argued that the world as it appears to our senses is merely a copy of immaterial, eternal Forms or Ideas, which alone truly exist. For Plotinus, the Ideas constitute the second level of reality (or 'hypostasis'), Intellect: this hypostasis comes from the One, by emanation, a type of derivation which brings no change to that from which the derivation takes place. Similarly, from Intellect emanates the third hypostasis, Soul, which is responsible for all that makes up the life of the universe, from the workings of the elements to human reasoning.

Plotinus' successors kept and elaborated this three-layered metaphysical structure, but it was his pupil, Porphyry (*c.*232–305) who gave the late ancient tradition its distinctive character. Whereas Plotinus had regarded Aristotle with reserve, Porphyry accepted his thinking as well as Plato's, contending that Plato wrote about the intelligible world and Aristotle about the everyday world perceptible through the senses, so that the two spoke in harmony, despite their apparent disagreements.

Porphyry therefore made Aristotle's works, including his logic, part of the Platonic curriculum, and the two great Platonic schools, at Athens and Alexandria, followed his lead. Although Plato's dialogues (and some mystical, pagan religious texts) were officially the culmination of the course, there was room for philosophers, such as Ammonius of Alexandria (d. 517–26), who concentrated on expounding Aristotle. The School of Athens flourished in the 5th century, an unreservedly pagan institution in an increasingly monolithically Christian Empire. Only in 529 did the Christian Emperor, Justinian, close it down.

Five originators of the medieval traditions

Five thinkers, each with strong links to late ancient Platonism and (except for one) to the Platonic schools, were founding figures for the medieval traditions.

Augustine (354–430), son of a Christian mother and pagan father, who became a bishop in Roman North Africa and the most influential of all Latin Christian writers, grew up in a world where the relationship between pagan philosophy and Christianity was conflicted. He was schooled in the Latin literary classics in preparation for a lucrative career as a rhetorician, but his encounter with Latin translations of Plotinus and Porphyry set him on the path to conversion, vividly recorded in his *Confessions*. His thinking continued to reflect this Platonism, yet, as it matured, it stressed the gulf between Christianity and Roman

civilization, and the corrupt, fallen state of humankind. Although his writings are unsystematic and often linked to questions of Christian doctrine or take the form of Biblical commentary, Augustine reflected deeply and originally about many philosophical themes, such as time, scepticism, the will, evil, and human freedom.

Unlike Augustine, Boethius (*c.*475/7–*c.*525/6) was trained in Greek as well as Latin and had access to material from the Platonic schools. Like Ammonius, he had a special interest in logic: he translated almost all Aristotle's logical works, and he wrote commentaries on them and logical textbooks, making this late ancient scholastic tradition available to Latin readers. A set of short theological works showed how these logical ideas and techniques could be applied to thinking about Christian doctrine. But, above all, Boethius became famous for his last work, the *Consolation of Philosophy*, written in prison under sentence of death on a trumped-up charge of treason. Drawing on Stoic and Platonic themes, the *Consolation* aims to provide a purely philosophical, reasoned vindication of divine providence, even in the face of the apparent injustice its author is suffering. It also develops an influential solution to the problem of reconciling God's foreknowledge with human freedom (see Chapter 8).

'Pseudo-Dionysius' (late 5th century), as he is called, was someone, probably a Syrian monk, who issued a set of writings under the name of Dionysius, the learned Athenian converted by St Paul (Acts 17:16–34). They were widely read for the next millennium, both in Byzantium and in Latin translation. They are based on Proclus. In Proclus' system, Plotinus' three hypostases are themselves divided and subdivided into groups of three, and the pagan gods are placed in this elaborate hierarchy. Pseudo-Dionysius took over the system, simplifying and Christianizing it, replacing gods with angels and the ecclesiastical hierarchy.

John Philoponus (c.490–570s) was another Syrian Christian. He studied under Ammonius at the School of Alexandria, but in his later years he used his Aristotelian training against Aristotle, in a series of works in Greek and Syriac, rejecting central aspects of his physical theory. For example, he used Aristotle's argument that it is impossible to traverse an infinite number of things as an argument against Aristotle's fundamental view, unacceptable to Christians, that the world has no beginning: if so, he objected, then there must have been an infinite number of changes before this fire which is burning now could come into existence—and that is impossible, according to Aristotle himself. Philoponus, who wrote in Greek and Syriac, was not read in the Byzantine tradition (where his branch of Christianity was considered heretical) nor, directly, in the Latin tradition, but he was an important figure, known as 'John the Grammarian', in Arabic philosophy.

Sergius of Resh'aynā (d. 536), also a Syriac Christian, knew Ammonius' logical teaching through Philoponus' versions of the lectures. He is regarded as the founder of the Syriac logical tradition which, through the work of Syriac Christian teachers and translators (from Greek to Syriac and Arabic), stands at the beginning of Greek-based philosophy in Arabic. Sergius also contributed to the Platonic side of the Syriac tradition, as the translator into Syriac of pseudo-Dionysius.

Philosophy in the continuity and collapse of the Roman Empire

These five figures all lived in what was still, culturally, the ancient world, though a Christianized one. In the east the Roman Empire, with its capital at Byzantium, continued; the people we call 'Byzantines' thought of themselves as Romans. There the most powerful philosopher of the 7th century, Maximus the Confessor (580–662), continued the tradition of pseudo-Dionysius. Following Proclus, pseudo-Dionysius had stressed how God himself is unknowable and can be described only negatively.

Taking this idea further, Maximus argues that God is not a thing at all, and that it is only by allowing things to participate in him that he creates himself.

Although familiar with logic and deeply influenced by Platonic themes, Maximus held the pagan tradition of philosophy in low esteem. His two successors in the Greek tradition, John of Damascus (d. before 754), and Photius, Patriarch of Constantinople (820–91), who also developed philosophically informed theological systems, took a different view. John prefaced his *summa* of theology with (a rather elementary) introduction. Photius assembled a vast *Bibliotheca*, a collection of extracts from ancient authors, including philosophers, and elsewhere he discussed logical problems, with a view to putting logic to use in theology.

By contrast, in the west, Roman political control and institutions were already crumbling in the 6th century. North Africa had been lost to the Vandals shortly after Augustine's death, and Boethius' Italy was under the rule of the Goths. Further barbarian invasions followed, and it was not until the late 8th century, with the peace, stability, and cultural revival brought by Charlemagne, crowned Emperor on Christmas Day 800, that the Latin tradition of philosophy began to be revived. The English scholar, Alcuin (d. 804), Charlemagne's protégé, compiled the first medieval Latin logical handbook, and students in his circle dabbled with philosophical themes and arguments they found in Augustine, Boethius, and the *Timaeus*, the one work of Plato's available in (an incomplete) Latin translation.

John Scottus Eriugena (fl. c.850–70), who worked at the court of Charlemagne's grandson, Charles the Bald, was a vastly more original and ambitious philosopher. Eriugena's special admiration was for the tradition of Greek Christian thought. He learned Greek and translated the whole pseudo-Dionysian corpus, works by Maximus the Confessor, and one by an earlier, philosophically

minded Church Father of the 4th century, Gregory of Nyssa. In his masterpiece, the *Periphyseon*, Eriugena systematized and greatly extended Maximus' thinking, helped by his study of Aristotelian logic and often in dialogue with Augustine, whose work he had also read carefully. Eriugena's God, utterly unknowable and indefinable, is both uncreated and creating—constituting himself as an object of knowledge through the universe which is, ultimately, just an appearance of Him—and also uncreated and uncreating, when seen as the end to which all things return (see Figure 2).

In the 10th and 11th centuries, philosophy continued to be studied in the Latin West on the basis of a small number of ancient and late ancient texts: a few works of Aristotelian logic, Roman popularizations of Platonism, the *Timaeus*, and Boethius—his commentaries, textbooks, theological treatises, and the *Consolation*. The most remarkable thinker of the period, Anselm (1033–1109), spent much of his life in a Norman monastery, before he became Archbishop of Canterbury. Unlike most medieval writers, he rarely cites authorities. He learned from Aristotle, Augustine, and Boethius, but—a finer philosophical mind than any of them except, perhaps, Aristotle—he rarely accepts their positions uncritically. His writings, often in the form of dialogues, though concerned with Christian doctrine, explore some of the most difficult issues in moral psychology, the philosophy of action and the philosophy of religion. His famous argument for God's existence is part of an extended exercise in a discipline he himself invented: perfect-being theology—the attempt to deduce rationally what God's attributes must be given that he is omniperfect.

The beginning of Arabic philosophy

The greatest of all the geopolitical changes at the end of antiquity was the rise of Islam. By 700 Muslim armies had conquered Syria, Iraq, and Egypt (territories which had belonged to Byzantium), the Persian Empire, much of North Africa, and what had been the Christian Visigothic Kingdom of Spain.

2. Illumination in a 12th-century manuscript of Honorius
Augustodunensis' *Clavis Physicae*, an abbreviation of John Scottus
Eriugena's *Periphyseon*, which depicts Eriugena's conception of the
universe.

For philosophy, however, the result was not a break with the ancient
tradition, but the very opposite. The School of Alexandria had
survived, along with its books, until the town fell to the Muslims in
641. Between the late 8th and early 10th century, in the first of the

great translation movements which gave shape to medieval philosophy, almost all these philosophical and scientific texts were put into Arabic. Some of the most important translators were Syriac-speaking Christians. The philosophical works translated included almost the whole of Aristotle and many commentaries on him from the Platonic schools and late ancient Aristotelians, such as Alexander of Aphrodisias (active *c.* AD 200), as well as work extracted from Plotinus (confusingly called the *Theology of Aristotle*) and from the 5th-century Platonist Proclus (*The Book of the Pure Good*). Plato himself was known through translations of epitomes.

From the early 9th century some scholars in Islam consciously set out to continue this Greek tradition of what they called *falsafa*. But they were not the only, nor the first, philosophers in Islam. From the early 700s Muslim scholars began to engage in *kalām*, a type of philosophical discussion based on Quranic problems and questions, but probably also influenced by some knowledge of ancient Greek ideas (though not by study of the texts) and the need to defend Islam against the philosophically trained Syriac Christians.

Both those who attached themselves to the Greek tradition and the earliest dominant school of *kalām*, the Mu'tazilites, were seeking, in different ways, a rational understanding of their world and their religion, and both groups were fostered by the new 'Abbāsid dynasty (established 750). The Mu'tazilites placed great emphasis on the power of human reason to understand divine justice, and they emphasized God's absolute unity. Mostly they were atomists, and they seem consciously to have rejected the Aristotelian picture of a stable world made of substances belonging to certain, fixed natural kinds (such as humans, dogs, roses, and stones) for one in which, under God's aegis, atoms are bound together as things by accidents.

The first of the great exponents of *falsafa*, al-Kindī (*c.*801–66) seems deliberately to have presented his Greek-inspired thinking as an alternative to *kalām*—a different and better way of solving the same,

ultimately theological problems, within the framework of Islam. Al-Kindī was especially influenced by the more Platonic translations, such as the *Theology of Aristotle*. It would be wrong, though, to describe him as a Platonist. Rather, he was a polymath, who ranged over mathematics, music, and all the sciences, fascinated by the riches of a library he and his contemporaries had yet to absorb.

By contrast, al-Fārābī (*c*.870–950/1) was a determined follower of the ancient, Aristotelian tradition, and he traced his own intellectual genealogy, teacher by teacher, back to Aristotle himself. Not only did he comment on Aristotle and, combining Aristotelian and Platonic metaphysics with Ptolemaic cosmology, develop a theory of emanation which strongly influenced medieval thinking about intellectual knowledge (see Figure 3, and Chapter 7). He also developed a Platonically tinged model of the perfect city (see Chapter 9), and an audacious theory of the relationship between Aristotelian demonstrative science and religion, which he believed sets out the same truths as science, but in a metaphorical form capable of being grasped by non-philosophers. Islam offers the best metaphorical representation, but only Aristotelian science gives the naked truth. Al-Fārābī was the central figure of a whole school of 'Baghdad Peripatetics', who concentrated, though not exclusively, on expounding and discussing Aristotle.

Al-Fārābī's Baghdad circle included Christians as well as Muslims. Jews too became fully assimilated into the culture of Islam, following its intellectual trends and writing in Arabic. Isaac Israeli (b. 850), for example, was, like al-Kindī, inspired mainly by Platonic works from late antiquity, while Saadia (882–942), head of the ancient Talmudic academy of Babylon, produced a type of Jewish *kalām*.

Ibn Sīnā (Avicenna; before 980–1037) admired al-Fārābī, but, born near Bukhara on the eastern extremity of Islam, he distinguished his approach sharply from that of the Baghdad Peripatetics. Where they aimed to paraphrase or interpret Aristotle, paragraph by paragraph,

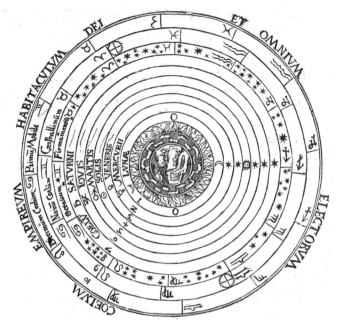

3. The Aristotelian–Ptolemaic universe, in an engraving from Peter Apian's *Cosmographia*, 1524.

with the help of the ancient commentaries, Avicenna set out to systematize the thought of Aristotle and his commentators, rearranging the elements and very often rethinking them. Unlike al-Fārābī, Avicenna does not try to trace a philosophical lineage back to the ancients. Rather than rely on a teacher, he could use his own ḥads, his power to form arguments, to seize on the truth in what he read, changing whatever was necessary. His favoured form of writing was, accordingly, the philosophical encyclopaedia, covering the whole Aristotelian curriculum according to his own reading of it. The longest of these works was called *The Cure*; the latest, and most influential in Islam, *Pointers and Reminders*, epitomized his teaching for initiates. Avicenna innovated in almost every field, from modal logic to the theory of universals (see

17

Chapter 6) and of body and mind. His most far-reaching development was his distinction—among things which, being eternal, are necessary (in Aristotle's sense)—between those things that are necessary through another, because they require a cause for their existence, and God, who alone is necessary in himself: the mere fact of what he is explains that he exists.

While *falsafa* flourished, *kalām* continued to develop. Al-'Asharī (d. 935/6) began his career as a Mu'tazilite, but abandoned some of the school's characteristic doctrines, while retaining its atomism and using it to emphasize God's complete power over everything—even (against the Mu'tazilites) human volition and action. The idea that God is the sole creator of everything, including human acts, was emphasized by al-Juwaynī (1028–85). But Juwaynī was also a reader of Avicenna, who introduced his notions of necessity and possibility into his theological discussion.

Juwaynī's outstanding pupil was al-Ghazālī (1058–1111), still revered as one of Islam's greatest religious thinkers. His studies and interests included not only Asharite *kalām*, but law, Sufism, and *falsafa*. His attitude to philosophy in the Greek tradition, and its leading exponent, Avicenna, was two-sided. He compiled a summary of Avicennian thought—the *Intentions of the Philosophers*—but only to attack it, thesis by thesis, in the *Incoherence of the Philosophers*; and he judged three of Avicenna's Aristotelian views, that the world is eternal, that God has no knowledge of particulars, and that there is no bodily resurrection, to be not merely wrong, but heretical. Yet he borrowed heavily from Avicenna's system, to the extent that some consider his metaphysical framework to be entirely Avicenna's, except that for al-Ghazālī the existent which is necessary of itself, God, acts, not out of necessity, but voluntarily.

Latin philosophy in the 12th century

In the Latin world, Paris, where the cathedral authorities allowed competing schools, became the outstanding intellectual centre in

the early 12th century, with masters and their followers in constant debate. The curriculum was much the same as that of the previous century and a half, with logic more important than ever; the few Aristotelian writings known, along with Boethius' commentaries and textbooks, were now thoroughly scrutinized. Theology, in a form highly influenced by the Masters' logical training, also came to be studied in the Paris schools. The result was a special, characteristically 12th-century way of thinking, based on logical and linguistic analysis, perhaps closer to contemporary analytic philosophy than the more fully Aristotelian philosophy which would replace it.

Peter Abelard (1079–1142), the most famous 12th-century Parisian teacher, made his name as a logician. He also advanced a controversial theory of universals (see Chapter 6), and he went on to develop a wide-ranging ethico-theological system, in which God cannot choose between alternatives, because he must always do whatever is best, but humans are free and will be judged according to their intentions in following divine law, revealed or as naturally known to everyone. A different, but equally sophisticated and highly distinctive approach to language, logic, metaphysics, and their relations to God was taken by Gilbert of Poitiers (c.1085/90–1154). In the second half of the century, the followers of Abelard, Gilbert, and other important early 12th-century Masters formed rival schools, each with its own proclaimed logical and metaphysical principles.

In theology, the main contention involved two parties. There were those who based their method broadly on Gilbert of Poitiers, who himself was influenced by Boethius (his most important work is a commentary on Boethius' theological treatises). A different approach to theology, however, had been pioneered in Laon at the turn of the century, and developed by Abelard. The collections of views or 'Sentences' written by these theologians looked at contentious points of doctrine and tried, often through conceptual analysis, to reconcile apparently conflicting authoritative texts

about them. It was this second approach which was adopted in 13th-century theology, and the *Sentences*, written by Peter the Lombard, Bishop of Paris, in the 1150s—based on Augustine, but influenced by contemporaries including Abelard—became the textbook for university theology.

Some thinkers had different interests. William of Conches (d. after 1155), who probably worked outside Paris, concentrated on expounding texts such as Boethius' *Consolation* and Plato's *Timaeus*. He was particularly concerned with physical science, and saw Plato, rightly interpreted, as an authority in this field. Bernardus Silvestris dramatized the *Timaeus* in a work written in prose and verse; Adelard of Bath and Hermann of Carinthia looked towards Arabic culture for new scientific and mathematical knowledge; and, in writings associated with Thierry of Chartres, Boethius' Platonism was given a numerological, and sometimes even mystical, twist.

Muslim and Jewish philosophy in the Islamic West

In the late eleventh and twelfth centuries, the Islamic West—North Africa and Spain—developed its own philosophical culture. While Ibn Ṭufayl (before 1110–85) looked to Avicenna (see Chapter 9), Ibn Bājja (d. 1139) and Ibn Rushd (Averroes; c.1126–98) continued the Baghdad tradition of Aristotelianism. Averroes was, indeed, the most thorough of all the Arabic exegetes of Aristotle, commenting on the whole range of his known works—usually more than once and employing a variety of approaches, ranging from epitome to the 'great' commentaries (on five texts, including the *Metaphysics* and *On the Soul*), in which he examines Aristotle's text minutely, paragraph by paragraph.

Averroes was also the most determined to return to an authentic understanding of Aristotle, stripping him of Platonic accretions, and asserting that Muslims who were intellectually capable of it were duty-bound to study Aristotelian science. He counter-attacked al-Ghazālī by questioning the value of *kalām* in his *Incoherence of the*

Incoherence, and at the same time distanced himself from al-Ghazālī's own target, Avicenna, in the name of authentic Aristotelianism—and yet this very desire to grasp Aristotle's real meaning led him to an idiosyncratic and controversial reading of *On the Soul* (see Chapter 7). Averroes had almost no readers in later Islam, but many among Jews and Christians, and much of his work is preserved only in Hebrew or Latin.

The outstanding achievements of Jewish philosophy written in Arabic were products of this distinctive West Islamic culture. Solomon ibn Gabirol (1021/2–57/8), who spent most of his life in Saragossa, was a Hebrew poet, but wrote his only-surviving philosophical work, the *Fountain of Life*, in Arabic. Although heavily influenced by Platonism, Solomon did not conceive of things as emanating necessarily from the One, but as being produced by God's will; and he insisted on the presence of matter, which was made by God, at every level of the created universe. The first Jewish thinker to adopt a more Aristotelian approach, looking back to al-Fārābī, was Ibn Daud, in the mid-12th century. He was eclipsed by his contemporary Moses ben Maimon (Maimonides; Rambam, 1138–1204). Like the other two, Maimonides was a product of Andalusian Islamic culture, but he had to flee, eventually to Egypt, when the Almohad rulers began to persecute non-Muslims.

In his two great rabbinical works, the commentary on the Mishna (in Arabic) and the *Mishneh Torah* ('Second Law'), in Hebrew, Maimonides puts forward Aristotelianism as adapted by al-Fārābī and takes a view similar to his about the relationship between religion, for him Judaism, and Aristotelian science. The truths expressed openly by Aristotle were known, he contended, in the scriptural and rabbinic traditions, but expressed in metaphorical form. By the time he wrote the *Guide of the Perplexed*, however, his view had become more complicated. He now recognized that there were fundamental differences between an Aristotelian view of God as a being acting necessarily in an eternal universe and the

Jewish conception of a creator God, acting voluntarily. Although some themes in the *Guide* are clear—such as the strict negative theology and the attack on *kalām* arguments, the solution to this central problem is open to different interpretations. Did Maimonides give up important elements in Aristotelianism, or did he merely appear to do so and, through a subtle system of hints and self-contradictions, reject, though not openly, the literal truth of cherished aspects of Jewish belief?

Philosophy and *kalām* in the Islamic East after Avicenna

The distinctive philosophical culture of the Islamic West disappeared when, in the early 13th century, the Christians reconquered almost all of Muslim Spain. In the Islamic East, philosophy developed differently, partly at least because of the strong influence of al-Ghazālī. By choosing Avicenna as the object of his attack on philosophy, he helped to canonize him as *the* philosophical authority (rather than Aristotle); by labelling three of the philosophers' doctrines as 'unbelief' he paradoxically gave Muslims licence to adopt any of the philosophers' other views; and through his own adoption of Avicennian metaphysics, he set a fashion for future *kalām* theologians.

The philosophical tradition was, then, dominated by Avicenna, through imitation or by reaction, until the end of the 12th century. Avicenna's pupil, Bahmanyār (d. 1067), and his pupil, Al-Lawkarī (d. 1123/4), wrote philosophical encyclopaedias based on his work. By contrast with these Avicennians, in his *Book of Evidence* Abū-l-Barakāt al-Baghdādī (b. *c.*1077) attacked not only a number of Aristotelian physical principles, but, by subjecting each of them to doubt, many of Avicenna's positions.

Al-Baghdādī influenced another critic of Avicenna in the following century, Suhrawardī, executed on Saladin's orders in 1191, when he was not yet forty. Suhrawardī had already written prolifically,

and in the following centuries his 'philosophy of illumination' became an important strand in Islamic thinking, with an extensive commentary tradition of its own. Suhrawardī challenged the Aristotelian tradition, by claiming to incorporate ideas from ancient Chinese, Indian, Egyptian, and Persian philosophy, and through his central idea of a special sort of direct knowledge by presence, which makes possible a grasp of reality distinct from the imperfect knowledge achievable by discursive reasoning. He began as a follower of Avicenna, and he is an acute critic, from a Platonic perspective, of certain questionable aspects of his system, such as the distinction between essence and existence and the Aristotelian confidence in our ability to provide definitions.

Chapter 3
A map of later medieval philosophy

Earlier and later medieval philosophy

It was suggested in Chapter 1 that it is best to think of medieval philosophy as covering a very long period, stretching from roughly 200 to 1700 (the Long Middle Ages). Within this millennium and a half, the year 1200 marks an important break across all four traditions, so that, despite many continuities, the division into earlier medieval philosophy up to the end of the 12th century, and later medieval philosophy after it, is more than an arbitrary one (Figure 4).

The Latin tradition was transformed in the 13th century by the rise of the universities of Paris and Oxford and the reception of almost all Aristotle's works, along with a good deal of Arabic philosophy. After Maimonides died in 1204, Jewish philosophy, which had previously been written in Arabic and within the milieu of Islamic culture, flourished mainly among Jews living in Christian Europe and writing in Hebrew. In the same year, the Crusaders took Constantinople and set up a kingdom there: as a result, Byzantine philosophy was heavily influenced by Latin writing, or by reaction against it. Further, the death of Averroes in 1198 marked the end not only of the distinctive intellectual culture of Islamic Spain (as explained in Chapter 2) but also of the tradition of *falsafa*. Philosophy continued to flourish in the

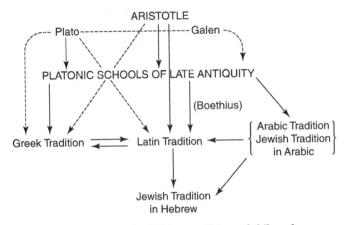

ARISTOTLE

--- Plato --------------------------- Galen ---

PLATONIC SCHOOLS OF LATE ANTIQUITY

(Boethius)

Greek Tradition ⇄ Latin Tradition ← { Arabic Tradition / Jewish Tradition in Arabic }

Jewish Tradition in Hebrew

4. The relations between the different traditions of philosophy.

Islamic East, but in a form already partly developed there by Avicenna's opponents and successors, which linked it much more closely to theology.

Translations into Latin and the universities

The years from about 1200 to 1250 witnessed a dramatic change in how philosophy was done in the Latin West, due to two factors: the second of the great medieval translation movements from Greek and Arabic into Latin, and the establishment of universities at Paris and Oxford (see Chapter 5).

The translation movement had begun in the 12th century, but it was only in the 13th century that the new translations started to be widely used. Beginning with the work of James of Venice between 1130 and 1150, Aristotle's texts were translated directly from the Greek. For some of Aristotle's work, indirect translations made from the Arabic had to be used in the 13th century, but, thanks to William of Moerbeke, by 1286 the whole of Aristotle was available in close, accurate Latin versions, along with some of the late ancient commentaries. Although this Aristotelian corpus

would be the centre of the curriculum, Platonic writings were not overlooked: the *Book of the Pure Good* was translated as the *Book of Causes* and was already being used in the 1170s; and William of Moerbeke translated directly the book from which it was adapted, Proclus' *Elements of Theology*. Along with pseudo-Dionysius' works, which were retranslated in the 12th century, these writings provided a Platonic strand important for some thinkers, even convinced Aristotelians, such as Albert the Great and Thomas Aquinas (who commented on both the *Book of Causes* and pseudo-Dionysius). Plato's own *Meno* and *Phaedo* were also translated, but they were almost entirely ignored.

Translations from the Arabic were important less for providing Aristotle's text than because they brought *falsafa* and Jewish philosophy from Islam to the Latin world: the two main centres were Toledo (in the mid- to late 12th century), and Sicily in the early 13th century. By about 1230, large parts of Avicenna's *Cure* (some of the logic, and the sections on metaphysics and the soul), some work by al-Fārābī, al-Ghazālī's *Intentions of the Philosophers*, a whole variety of Averroes' commentaries, and Ibn Gabirol's *Fountain of Life* had been translated from the Arabic, and Maimonides' *Guide* from its Hebrew translation.

The university theologians, 1200–1350

The best known of all medieval philosophers were theologians who studied and taught, at least for some of their lives, at the universities of Paris (Thomas Aquinas and Duns Scotus) and/or Oxford (Scotus again, and William of Ockham). They belonged to the two religious orders, the Dominicans (Aquinas) and the Franciscans (Scotus and Ockham), which dominated university theology.

The stereotypical picture, presented at the beginning of this book, of Aquinas (*c*.1225–74), the most famous member of this trio, distorts Aquinas' own aims and achievements as much as it does

medieval philosophy as a whole. Aquinas was influenced by Avicenna, especially at the beginning of his career. But, although he strongly rejected his view of the intellect (see Chapter 7), Aquinas' strongest affinity was with Averroes. Like Averroes, he thought that, properly understood, Aristotle was right about most philosophical questions, though unlike him he saw theology as completing Aristotelian science rather than being replaced by it. In order to share and improve his close knowledge of Aristotle, late in his career Aquinas set about writing detailed commentaries, near in style to Averroes' 'great' commentaries, on a number of the works. He clung to what he believed were Aristotle's true views even where, as with the position that there is only one substantial form in a substance, they made it harder for him to explain features of Christian belief.

Many of his contemporaries thought that Aquinas went too far in accepting Aristotelian positions. Although he was (at least ostensibly) supported by his fellow Dominicans, many of his views were widely rejected, and a number of treatises correcting his errors were written. It was only in the 16th century that many in the Church began to regard him as their principal authority in philosophy and theology, and that his *Summa Theologiae* started to be used as a theology textbook; and only in 1879, with Pope Leo XIII's bull *Aeterni Patris*, that Aquinas was made to stand for a supposedly unified scholastic philosophy, which Catholics were urged to cultivate in order to combat the hostile trends in contemporary thought.

Duns Scotus (1265/6–1308) was also a careful and respectful reader of Aristotle, whose ideas were even better known by the turn of the 13th century, but he belonged to the Franciscan tradition, championed in Aquinas' time by Bonaventure (1221–74), which emphasized, in opposition to Aristotle, the active power of human intellect and will. Guided by this tendency, along with a wish to underline God's complete freedom, Scotus proceeded to rethink almost every theological and philosophical issue on which

27

he touched, from universals and individuation (see Chapter 6) to the meaning of possibility and necessity (see Chapter 8), epistemology, and ethics. He tended to explain problems by discovering what he claimed are real, but hidden, features of reality, which are distinguishable only after very careful investigation. William of Ockham (c.1288–1347) shared Scotus' fundamental aims, but was sharply critical of this metaphysics. Through a theory of mental language and its relation to the world, he believed that could provide a satisfactory explanation for how things are, leaving a drastically simplified, nominalist world of individual things and their qualities (see Chapter 6).

From the mid-13th century, there was a constant succession of highly trained philosopher-theologians, and many of them produced their own, distinctive answers to the central problems of the time. There is space to mention only a very few of them. Alexander of Hales (c.1185–1245) established the Franciscan tradition of university theology; the vast summa, attributed to him but written by his pupils, is the most impressive work of philosophical theology from the first half of the 13th century. Albert the Great (1200–80), who worked mainly in Cologne, was Aquinas' teacher, but outlived him. He was a pioneer in using the newly translated material and boasted of his extensive knowledge of ancient and Arabic thought. The system of emanation he found in al-Fārābī and Avicenna particularly attracted him, and he continued to treat the *Book of Causes* as providing the completion of Aristotle's metaphysics even after Aquinas had shown that it was derived from Proclus' *Elements of Theology*. A distinctive, German school of theologians, including Dietrich of Freiberg (c.1250–1318/20) and Meister Eckhart (1260–1327/8), looked back especially to Albert.

The most influential Paris theologian of the years immediately after Aquinas was Henry of Ghent (c.1217–93); Scotus developed many of his distinctive positions in opposition to him. By contrast, Peter John Olivi (1248–98), perhaps because of his originality and

daring, enjoyed little prestige and for a period was forbidden to teach; he anticipated a number of the ideas about knowledge and the will which Scotus would develop. In Oxford, Ockham was not the only brilliant philosopher of the 1320s and 1330s. His contemporary, Walter Chatton (c.1290–1343), who defended Scotism, argued with him, while the Dominican, Robert Holcot (c.1290–1349), adopted many Ockhamist ideas and wrote about them for a wider audience, outside the universities.

The Arts Masters and non-university philosophy in Western Europe, 1200–c.1400

The theologians were all highly trained in Aristotelianism, but it was among the Masters in the much larger Faculty of Arts (see Chapter 5) that its votaries were found: Masters who saw their vocation as understanding and expounding Aristotle, using reason and not discussing revealed truth. The most famous of the mid-13th-century Paris Arts Masters was Siger of Brabant, whom Dante places in Paradise (X, 136) along with Boethius, Aquinas, and Albert the Great. Siger, however, was condemned by Aquinas and others for adopting Averroes' views about the intellect. His contemporary, Boethius of Dacia, provided one of the clearest and most sophisticated defences of the Arts Masters' duty to follow Aristotelian science, even when it conflicts with Christian doctrine. Whenever an Arts Master makes an assertion, it is to be understood as qualified by the principles of the particular discipline he is practising. When, for example, a natural scientist declares, as he must in accord with Aristotle, that the world has no beginning, what he is really saying is: *according to the principles of natural science*, the world has no beginning. He does not therefore contradict the Christian doctrine that, absolutely speaking, the world does have a beginning.

In early 14th-century Paris, John of Jandun (1285/9–1328) continued this devotion to an explanation of Aristotle in his own terms, distinguished strictly from the demands of Christian

doctrine. He knew Averroes' commentaries much better than his predecessors, and became renowned as an Averroist; but he was not a slavish follower, and he allowed recent developments among the theologians to shape some of his interpretations of Aristotle. John's colleague, Marsilius of Padua, applied to political philosophy a similarly sharp distinction between the spheres of reason and faith in his *Defender of the Peace* (1324) (see Chapter 9).

Up until the 16th century, Arts Masters, especially in Italy, but also in late 14th-century Erfurt and 15th-century Krakow, promoted an Averroistic Aristotelianism, using Averroes' view of the intellect to mark out very clearly the distinction between their reason-based teaching and Christian doctrine. Others rejected this position of Averroes, but were equally keen to keep their sphere separate from that of the theologians. John Buridan (*c*.1300–60) is the most important of them.

Probably (along with Abelard) the finest logician of the entire Latin Middle Ages, Buridan taught for forty years at the Paris Arts Faculty, introducing a brand of nominalism which achieved with less bluster the same objectives as Ockham's: a drastic thinning of the ontological inventory in favour of purely mental, linguistic distinctions. Although Buridan was willing to use his skills to reject arguments made against positions required by Christian doctrine, he was very clear in maintaining that there are no rational arguments for the creation of the world *ex nihilo* or the immortality of the soul.

Although after 1200 philosophy in Europe was studied mainly at universities and in Latin, there were exceptions. Ramon Llull (1232–1315), a Majorcan without a university education, produced a vast oeuvre, in Latin, Catalan, and Arabic, elaborating an eccentric form of logic, attacking Averroism and trying to persuade Muslims to convert. Eckhart proposed some of his most audacious ideas in sermons given in German to laypeople. In his

Divine Comedy, Dante (1265–1321) treats ideas taken from his reading of Aristotle, Aquinas, Albert the Great, and other philosophers; his *Convivio* is an independent philosophical treatise, close to the thinking of the Arts Masters; and his *Monarchia* is perhaps the most coherent and daring work of Latin political philosophy from the Middle Ages (see Chapter 9). Humanism—the movement to restore Latin to its classical form and elegance, learn Greek, and value the full range of literature and philosophy from the ancient world—had its origins outside the universities, but it was not, despite the antagonism of its most famous early exponent, Petrarch (Francesco Petrarca, 1304–74), in tension with them.

Later Byzantine philosophy

In Byzantium, there was a tradition of commentary on Aristotle that went back to the ancient schools. It suffered from two big problems. One was external. Scholars who devoted themselves to understanding texts by pagan philosophers were likely to find themselves accused of 'Hellenism' and condemned as heretics. While Michael Psellos (1018–96) managed to avoid condemnation, despite his interest in the ostentatiously pagan writings of the late Platonists, neither his pupil John Italos, nor Eustratius of Nicaea (*c*.1050–*c*.1120) escaped it, although both concentrated on Aristotle. The fear that any of these men were trying to revive the pagan Greek heritage seems to have been entirely misplaced, but in the case of Gemistos Plethon (*c*.1360–1454), a devoted follower of Plato and the late ancient Platonists, it would have been justified.

The theologically orientated tradition which went back to pseudo-Dionysius and Maximus the Confessor was continued by Gregory Palamas (1296–1359), a monk of Mount Athos. Palamas insisted on the complete unknowability of God, even to the blessed in heaven. But, he went on, God does manifest himself, and his activities can be known in this life by those who engage in a special sort of prayer. Palamas was opposed by writers such as

Barlaam of Calabria (c.1290–1348), who favoured an approach nearer to that of the Latins. Ever since the Latin Empire of Constantinople (1204–61), Latin philosophy and theology had started to be studied in Byzantium, with Greek translations being made of works by Augustine, Boethius, Aquinas, and other scholastic theologians. Barlaam, however, took a far more sceptical attitude to the possibility of theological knowledge than Aquinas, even going as far as to suggest that the doctrinal differences between the Eastern and Western Churches could be settled by agreeing that they concerned matters about which humans are unable to know the truth.

Jewish philosophy, 1200–1350

Jewish philosophy in Arabic did not cease with Maimonides' death and the end of the tradition based in Western Islamic culture. Besides some mystically inclined thinking, there were Jewish philosophers so integrated into Arabic culture that they seem not to be distinctively Jewish at all. One of them, discussed earlier, was Abū-l-Barakāt al-Baghdādī. He converted to Islam at the end of his life, but his position as a Jew may well have been what enabled him to look at Avicennism from the outside and become its most influential critic. Another such integrated Jewish philosopher (who may also have finally converted to Islam) was Ibn Kammūna, who commented on Avicenna and Suhrawardī, and was a reader and correspondent of al-Ṭūsī's.

From the 13th century onwards, however, distinctively Jewish philosophy took place mainly in Hebrew, among the Jewish communities of Christian Europe, especially in southern France, Spain, and, later, Italy. It depended on the third of the great medieval translation movements: Maimonides' philosophical masterpiece, the *Guide of the Perplexed*, was translated into two different Hebrew versions almost as soon as it was written; a large amount of Averroes was also translated—Jewish thinkers tended to read and comment on Averroes' epitomes rather than on

Aristotle's texts themselves; al-Ghazālī's *Intentions of the Philosophers* and Ibn Ṭufayl's philosophical novel were also translated, along with some Avicenna, but his influence was limited.

The *Guide of the Perplexed* was a central, controversial text in these Jewish communities. In some of them, it was banned at times by those who thought Maimonides had accepted too much from Aristotelian science. By contrast, some thinkers, such as Albalag, in the second half of the 13th century, considered Maimonides far too ready to give way to the demands of religious doctrine; or, like Samuel ibn Tibbon, one of the *Guide*'s translators, they read the book as surreptitiously implying a far more radical, Aristotelian doctrine than it literally stated. Albalag followed Aristotle as transmitted by Averroes, and others, such as Moses of Narbonne (*c*.1300–after 1362), took up Averroism even more directly.

The most wide-ranging and innovative of these philosophers was Levi ben Gershom ('Gersonides'; 1288–1344) a logician, prolific commentator (mainly of Averroes' commentaries), and author of *The Wars of the Lord*, in which he re-explored many of the philosophical problems that had troubled Maimonides, using Averroes but also Avicenna and not hesitating to press forward his own arguments, sometimes to very radical conclusions—as on God's foreknowledge (see Chapter 8).

Arabic philosophy, 1200–1600

Like his shorter-lived coeval, Suhrawardī (discussed in Chapter 2), Ibn ʿArabī (1165–1240) is a celebrated figure in the Islamic intellectual tradition, and an influence on subsequent philosophers, but is often put at the edges of the history of philosophy, because of his opposition to Avicenna and Aristotle and the entire tradition of Greek philosophy, and his appeal to mysticism. Yet he expresses himself using philosophical terms.

A letter survives from Ibn ʿArabī to Fakhr al-Dīn al-Rāzī (c.1150–1210), the outstanding philosopher and theologian of the time, recognizing his learning but advising him that true wisdom can be gained only through a non-discursive, mystical path. Al-Rāzī, whose work is characterized by careful discussion and weighing up of different views and arguments, was probably unimpressed. He was the central figure in the process, inspired by al-Ghazālī, of bringing together Avicennian philosophy and *kalām*, and of bringing together Avicenna's followers and his critics.

As well as commentaries on Avicenna's *Pointers and Reminders* and on the Quran, he wrote treatises both in the *kalām* tradition and philosophical encyclopaedias in the tradition of Avicenna, and he allowed discussions associated with *kalām* into the philosophical works and philosophical topics into his *kalām*. Although Avicenna is both a model and an authority, he is criticized, both in the light of al-Rāzī's own (sophisticated and much adapted) Ashʿarite position and the views of al-Baghdādī. Especially important was his *Compendium of Philosophy*, where he reworked the traditional divisions of philosophy: it exerted a strong influence on treatises in the *kalām* tradition such as the *Book of Stations in Kalām* by al-Ījī (d. 1355), which was widely used for centuries in *kalām* teaching, gathering its own tradition of commentaries.

Al-Rāzī's work also provided a starting point for more specifically philosophical *summas*. Al-Abharī (d. 1265), said to be a pupil of al-Rāzī's, and his pupil, al-Kātibī (d. 1276), wrote influential encyclopaedic accounts of philosophy, looking back to al-Rāzī rather than Avicenna himself (who has almost vanished from the picture), innovating structurally and in some respects returning to subject divisions closer to Aristotle's, as well as adding elements derived from Suhrawardī into their discussion.

The lifetimes of these two men coincided with the Mongol invasions, but they were able to work on logic, philosophy, and

astronomy in the congenial atmosphere of the Marāgha Observatory, set up in 1259, thanks to the political abilities and flexibility with regard to faith and allegiance of al- Ṭūsī (1201–74). Al- Ṭūsī, a prolific and brilliant theologian, moral and political thinker, logician, mathematician, scientist, and, perhaps above all, astronomer, is especially important in philosophy for the commentary he wrote on *Pointers* where, although making some criticisms, he is often concerned to defend Avicenna against al-Rāzī's attacks. In the following centuries, ways of approaching Avicenna remained at the centre of philosophical discussion—as, for instance, in the protracted debate between al-Dawānī (d. 1501), whose reading was influenced by Suhrawardī (on whom he commented) and Ibn 'Arabī, and the al-Dashtakīs, father (d. 1498) and son (d. 1541), who preferred to stay closer to the original.

Some of the most original thinking of the whole period, however, was the work of a traditionalist theologian, Ibn Taymiyya (1263–1328), who considered himself an opponent of philosophy, as well as of *kalām* and mysticism, such as Ibn 'Arabī's, all of which, he believed, led to heresy. He argued for a nominalism in which our grouping of things into supposedly natural kinds (humans, flowers, stones) is merely a matter of convenience, since there are no real essences on which to base such a classification, and he took a sceptical view of Aristotelian demonstrative argument.

Philosophy and theology in the universities, 1350–1600

Universities in the 15th century, especially in German-speaking lands and France, were dominated by the so-called *Wegestreit*: the conflict between those who wanted to continue following the *via moderna* of nominalists, such as Ockham and Buridan, and those who favoured the *via antiqua*, a return to the teachings of 13th-century Masters such as Aquinas and Albert the Great. The conflict was not, as it might seem, about universals, but about whether philosophical teaching should be rigorously separated from

theology, especially for beginning students, as in the *via moderna*; or whether, as in the *via antiqua*, Aristotle should be used to give a defence of Catholic truth. Despite this concentration on the past (or perhaps through it), however, innovative thinking continued.

John Wyclif (*c.*1330–84) lived before the conflict. He, indeed, rejected the nominalism of his Oxford predecessors, but for his own, adventurous and idiosyncratic realist logic and metaphysics. In France, John Capreolus (*c.*1380–1444) opted for the *via antiqua* and set himself up as the defender of Thomas Aquinas, but he had to reshape Aquinas' work in order to make it answer problems which had not been envisaged in the 13th century. Heymeric of Campo (*c.*1395–1460), who taught at the new universities of Louvain and Cologne, looked back, rather, to Albert, but developed his own, systematic Albertian metaphysics.

In the north Italian universities, where arts were often a preparation for training in medicine, a tradition of Aristotelianism grew up from the end the 14th century. Paul of Venice (1368/9–1429) studied in Oxford and wrote a vast compendium of late medieval logic. Agostino Nifo (*c.*1470–1538) commented on the whole range of Aristotle (and also on Averroes' *Incoherence of the Incoherence*, which had been translated in the 14th century). Although, like almost all these Italian Arts Masters, he followed in the tradition of distinguishing their job of reason-based exposition of Aristotle from Christian doctrine, he became a fierce opponent of Pietro Pomponazzi (1462–1525), who argued that neither Aristotle nor reason supports the immortality of the soul (see Chapter 7). In the commentaries of men such as Jacopo Zabarella (1533–89), who taught at Padua, this sophisticated Aristotelianism continued through to the end of the century.

The last of the great theologians at Paris in the medieval tradition was a Scotsman, John Major (or Mair; 1467/9–1550), who was nominalist in his leanings. Whereas he taught theology in the customary way, by commenting on Peter the Lombard's *Sentences*, his pupil, Peter Crockaert, decided to use Aquinas' *Summa*

Theologiae as the text for commentary. This practice was followed by Francisco de Vitoria (*c.*1486–1546), the first of a succession of brilliant philosopher-theologians at the Spanish universities in the following century. The greatest of them all was Francisco Suárez (1548–1617). Although Suárez followed the Thomist direction of thinking favoured at the time, he was also strongly influenced too by Scotus and Ockham, and his careful, orderly sifting of every problem offers a nuanced account of the whole scholastic tradition along with solutions which are often strikingly original—as was his decision to write an independent treatise on metaphysics, breaking away entirely from Aristotle's text.

Humanism and Latin philosophy outside the universities

In the 15th and 16th centuries, there were great cultural changes in Western Europe, which according to many historians brought on a new epoch: the discovery and exploitation of America, the rise of Protestantism, and the growth of humanism, which led to a wave of new philosophical translations—of Plato and Platonists, and of ancient commentaries on Aristotle and Aristotle himself into more polished Latin. It may seem as if the 16th-century philosophers and theologians described earlier confined themselves to an isolated, anachronistic medieval world. On the contrary: Vitoria and his Spanish successors were deeply involved with the ethical questions raised by the Spanish conquests (Vitoria, indeed, all but ruled them illegitimate); and many of them, such as Suárez, were Jesuits, the shock troops of the Counter-Reformation response to Protestantism. Humanism was absorbed into the arts courses. Some of the philosophers learned Greek and all used the new translations so far as they judged useful, but they were understandably reluctant to abandon a framework and language which allowed them to approach most fundamental philosophical questions with clarity and sophistication. The attitude of Anglophone philosophers today to Continental philosophy offers an instructive parallel.

Outside the universities, there were thinkers more willing to philosophize according to the humanist ideals. Lorenzo Valla (1406–57) launched a (generally unsuccessful) attempt to reform Aristotelian logic, and he wrote on ethics in the verbose manner of Ciceronian dialogue. Marsilio Ficino (1433–99) devoted himself to translating and commenting on Plotinus and forging a consciously Platonic philosophy, which he advertised as being more supportive to Christian orthodoxy than Aristotelianism. By contrast, Giovanni Pico della Mirandola (1463–94) embarked on a fantastical project, designed to syncretize not just Aristotelianism and Platonism, but all the traditions of scholastic theology, Islamic thought, Zoroastrianism, and the Kabbala. Another, more restrained and accomplished, eclectic but with a voice distinctively his own, was Nicholas of Cusa (1401–64). Nicholas studied at Heidelberg but, as a high-flying papal diplomat, came to know Italian intellectuals and the translations of Plato being made at the time. He was especially attracted to negative theology (looking back to Eriugena as well as Proclus and the pseudo-Dionysius), and to the use of paradoxes such as that of a 'coincidence of opposites' in order to think about God.

Valla, Ficino, Pico, and Nicholas of Cusa are often described as 'Renaissance' philosophers, by contrast with 'medieval' ones. This label is a useful one when it is used to mark out these non-university philosophers, deeply influenced by humanism and the cultural fashions of *quattrocento* Italy, but not if it is treated as referring to a chronological period which came after medieval philosophy. As even this map of the subject shows, the material as a whole resists such a periodization.

Jewish philosophy, 1350–1600

Hasdai Crescas (*c.*1340–1410/11), leader of the Spanish Jews when their communities were under attack, was at once more audacious and more of a traditionalist than Gersonides. He defended

traditional Jewish belief by attacking Aristotle philosophically, finding powerful arguments against much of his physical and cosmological theory. He rejected the view, common in the Jewish tradition, which went back to both Maimonides and Averroes, that the highest happiness is open only to philosophers.

Crescas was very probably influenced by knowledge of Christian theology and philosophy (probably including some of Scotus' ideas). Gersonides, too, had probably been influenced at least in method by scholastically trained Latin scholars, with whom he could have spoken in the vernacular, and earlier, around 1300, in Italy there had even been a sort of Hebrew Thomism. In the 15th century, the influence of Christian thought on Jewish philosophers in Italy and Spain became strong and widespread. Elijah Delmedigo (c.1458–93), who taught at Padua and wrote philosophy in Hebrew and Latin, remained in many ways a rather old-fashioned Jewish Averroist, but one able to give a detailed critique of Aquinas. For Jews unable to read Latin, translations into Hebrew were made of Aristotle's own texts, from the Latin (sometimes from the new humanistic translations), and also of writings by Aquinas and his followers, texts by Scotists, and of logical works. Some Jewish thinkers took up the characteristic problems of scholastic theologians and their techniques for treating them, demonstrating a wide knowledge, direct and indirect, of texts by Arts Masters and university theologians.

When does medieval philosophy end?

The Byzantine tradition of philosophy has a fairly clear end, with the demise of the Eastern Empire after the fall of Constantinople in 1453. In the lands of Islam, the beginning of the 16th century marks a certain sort of break. By this time, there were three Muslim Empires, embracing most of the Islamic world: those of

the Ottoman Turks, the Mughals in India, and, most recent, of the Safavids in Persia. There was a tendency for philosophy to develop separately in each of the traditions—certainly this was the case for logic. Yet the underlying tradition was a continuation of the medieval one.

In Persia the central figure was Mullā Ṣadrā (Ṣadr al-Dīn Shīrāzī; c.1571–1636), a slightly older contemporary of Descartes. Mullā Ṣadrā draws on the mysticism of Ibn ʿArabī and the illuminationist philosophy of Suhrawardī, but maintains a strong commitment to rational argument and close links with the tradition that stretches back to Avicenna (on whose *Cure* he commented) and ultimately to Aristotle. His masterpiece, *Four Intellectual Journeys*, looks back at once to Avicenna, Ibn ʿArabī, and Fakhr al-Dīn al-Rāzī for its plan. His contemporary, Mīr Dāmād (d. 1630), continued a centuries-old debate, however, by countering Mullā Ṣadrā's mix of Avicenna with illuminationism and mysticism with a more faithful Avicennism. In the centuries which followed, the tradition continued. So, for instance, al-Rāzī's and al-Ṭūsī's commentaries on *Pointers* would be studied together until the 20th century, while (a sign that texts were not altogether confined to their geographical domains) Mullā Ṣadrā's commentary on an encyclopaedia by al-Abharī became a textbook in India in the 18th century.

The tradition of philosophy in Hebrew in Europe, concentrated by the 15th century in Italy and Spain, was abruptly uprooted from Spain when the Jews were expelled in 1492, but it survived for a while elsewhere: Isaac Abrabanel (d. 1508)—a powerful critic of many post-Maimonidean Jewish philosophers—went to live in Italy, and his son Judah, known as Leone Ebreo (c.1465—after 1521), combined Jewish and Platonic influences in his *Dialogues*, published (and probably written) in Italian. In the course of the 16th century, however, Italian Jews gradually turned their intellectual interests towards Kabbala. But the Spanish Jews who

went to the Turkish Empire continued philosophical work in Hebrew until about 1600.

According to the usual historiography, in Western Europe modern philosophy begins in the 17th century, with philosophers such as René Descartes (1596–1650), John Locke (1632–1704), Baruch Spinoza (1632–77), and Gottfried Wilhelm Leibniz (1646–1716), who sharply distinguished themselves from the scholastic tradition by their adoption of the new, mechanical physics and rejection of Aristotelian and Ptolemaic cosmology, and much of Aristotelian metaphysics.

Suárez, whose life overlaps with the first half of Descartes's, is considered to be the last of the scholastics (or—wrongly, as explained earlier—of a revived 'silver' scholasticism). A valuable advance on this received view has been made recently, as specialists have recognized the important scholastic influences on 'modern' philosophers. Descartes himself acknowledged reading Aquinas, and he is closer to the scholastic tradition than he likes to admit; Spinoza was influenced—some would say deeply—by Maimonides and Crescas; and Leibniz, a bibliographic omnivore, who was master of the whole tradition of the preceding centuries, reassimilated notions from Aristotelian metaphysics which Descartes had eliminated.

But historians of philosophy need to go further and reject the whole idea of a break, sometime early in the 17th century, between scholasticism and modern philosophy. In the universities the Aristotelian curriculum began to replaced only from the 1670s onwards (though in Protestant countries Aristotelian metaphysics had already been abandoned). Suárez can be seen, not as the last great writer in the scholastic tradition, but the first of a series of 'baroque' scholastic, though sometimes eclectic, philosophers, which includes, for instance, John of St Thomas (1589–1644), whose name indicates his doctrinal affiliations; the nominalistically inclined Thomist, Pedro Hurtado de Mendoza

5. A philosopher's church. The Duomo of Vigevano, designed by the
17th-century philosopher and polymath, Juan Caramuel y Lobkowitz.

(1578–1641), and his pupil, Rodrigo de Arriaga (1592–1667), the Scotist Bartolomeo Mastri (1602–75), and the polymathic innovator, Juan Caramuel y Lobkowitz (1606–82: see Figure 5). And the various different ways of setting out the philosophy curriculum within the 16th- and 17th-century university tradition would influence the direction philosophy took in different areas of Europe through to the 19th century.

Chapter 4
Fields of medieval philosophy

Logic

Partly as an inheritance from the Platonic schools, where the curriculum began with Aristotle's logical texts, logic was equally prominent in medieval philosophy as it is in contemporary analytical philosophy. As today, logic was both studied for itself with great technical sophistication, and used as a tool throughout philosophy, where it set the form of discussion. An important difference from now is that contemporary logicians develop mathematical systems which must then be translated into ordinary language. By contrast, medieval logic, although formal to a greater or lesser degree, never lost its links with ordinary language.

Aristotle's logical 'Organon' (literally 'tool') usually consisted of six texts: the *Categories* (really a treatise on basic metaphysics), which was prefaced by Porphyry's *Isagoge* ('Introduction'); *On Interpretation* (on semantics and the logical relations of statements); the *Prior Analytics* (which sets out his syllogistic: his system of logical argumentation); the *Posterior Analytics* (which uses syllogistic to elaborate a theory of scientific knowledge); *On Sophistical Refutations* (on fallacious arguments); and the *Topics* (on arguing from commonly accepted maxims). The other great logical tradition of antiquity, that of the Stoics, was almost entirely unknown, except for a muddled account in Boethius.

Although logic flourished in all four traditions, the only innovative Jewish logician so far known is Gersonides. Byzantine logic is hard to assess. There is a large, mostly unpublished literature of medieval Greek commentaries on Aristotelian logic, which are clearly very dependent on ancient models, and it has not yet been determined what, if any, elements are original. It is best, then, to concentrate on the achievements of Arabic and Latin logic. They make a fascinating comparison because, in this field, there was little influence of Arabic texts on Latin writers. It is therefore possible to see the extent to which the same ancient material is received and developed in two parallel traditions.

In the Arabic tradition, the whole of the Organon was available from early on; indeed, two further books by Aristotle were usually attached to it, the *Rhetoric* and the *Poetics*. The book which most impressed exponents of *falsafa* was the *Posterior Analytics*, because it taught them how to achieve certain knowledge through demonstration: syllogistic arguments with premises that are unchangingly true. They saw the rest of the extended Organon in the light of the *Posterior Analytics*, as setting out the other, less than fully scientific ways in which those without the intellectual gifts to become philosophers could to some extent grasp the truth. Sophistical syllogisms are, indeed, to be avoided by everyone, but poetical and rhetorical syllogisms are the right means for persuading the mass of people, by appeal in whole or part to their emotions, and it is this form of argumentation that, according to al-Fārābī and Averroes, is used by the Quran. Averroes considered that dialectical syllogisms—the sort treated in the *Topics*—were used by *kalām*-based writers, such as al-Ghazālī, but he queried their value, since they went beyond what was needed to persuade the masses, without offering properly scientific demonstrations.

Yet it was thanks especially to al-Ghazālī that logic, especially the formal syllogistic of the *Prior Analytics* which underlies the theory of demonstration, outlived *falsafa*. Al-Ghazālī helped to established logic as part of an Islamic religious education, essential not just for

theology but for law. Logic came, therefore, to be taught widely, and since the basis was Avicenna, not Aristotle's own texts, it did not seem like a foreign importation into Islam. In the 13th century, however, Avicenna's texts, though not his ideas, dropped out of the picture, and logic began to be taught through freshly written handbooks (the most famous of which was al-Kātibī's *Shamsiyya*), which themselves would become the objects of commentary. Avicenna had corrected and extended Aristotle's logic, exploring a far wider variety of forms of modal statements (about possibility and necessity) and their syllogisms than envisaged in the *Prior Analytics*. Subsequent logicians built on Avicenna's heritage, some strongly contesting his views, others supporting them. Within the overall framework of syllogistic inherited from Aristotle (whose own texts had long since disappeared from view), Arabic logicians continued to innovate well into the 18th century.

Until the 13th century, Latin logicians based their work on an abbreviated Organon (just the *Isagoge*, *Categories*, and *On Interpretation*; and, from *c.*1130, the *Sophistical Refutations*), supplemented with treatises by Boethius and others. They had very few other, non-logical ancient philosophical texts, and so it is perhaps not surprising that, on the basis of this syllabus, they developed a way of doing philosophy as a whole, using the *Isagoge* and *Categories* as the basis for their metaphysics, and *On Interpretation* for philosophy of language and mind (and in each case drawing from the rich selection of late ancient exegesis provided in Boethius' commentaries). Their method of logical and linguistic analysis was aided by the close ties between logic and grammar. The most brilliant of them, Peter Abelard, was also an innovator on the more technical side. Aristotelian syllogistic studies the logical relations of predicates, whereas Stoic logic had studied the logic of sentences. Inspired by Boethius' garbled account of the Stoics, it seems that Abelard reinvented a system of sentence logic.

From the 13th century onwards, Latin logicians studied the whole Organon (but not usually, as part of logic, the *Rhetoric* and *Poetics*).

They too were impressed by the idea of demonstration in the *Posterior Analytics*, but not as a way of marking out philosophers as against theologians; rather, they considered how theology itself could be considered an Aristotelian science. Unlike the Arabic logicians, they continued to comment closely on Aristotle's own texts until the 17th century. In their handbooks, however, they also treated at length various areas of logic—the so-called *logica modernorum* ('contemporary logic')—which had not been developed by Aristotle. These included various ways of studying ambiguity of meaning in natural language, an analysis of reference with the context of a sentence, and the development of various types of non-syllogistic deduction. The most famous of these handbooks was the *Treatise* (known as the *Summule logicales*) by Peter of Spain (*c.*1250). Buridan's great logical textbook, the *Summulae*, is written as a commentary on an adaptation of Peter's treatise, and Buridan's adapted text was itself the object of commentary in the 15th century.

Metaphysics

Almost every area of what is now called metaphysics was discussed in the Arabic and Latin traditions, and more sporadically in the Byzantine and Jewish ones. Except in *kalām*, the basic building blocks of the world were Aristotelian substances (such as a horse or a stone; and, for some, their universals, as in 'Pearl is a sort of *stone*') and accidents of the nine sorts distinguished in the *Categories* (quantity, quality, relation, where, when, posture, having, doing, being done to), but this framework left enormous room for different views and fresh questions. What degree of independence do accidents have? Are there real accidents in all the categories?

Things were seen to be structured both as substance and accident, and, even where the version of this doctrine in Aristotle's *Metaphysics* was not known, also as matter and substantial form (for instance, matter and the stone-ness which makes this thing into a stone), but there was controversy about whether everything

47

except God was composed in this way (a position taken by Ibn Gabirol which was much discussed by Christian scholars), and whether, as Aquinas strenuously denied, a substance could have more than one substantial form—is the form of a human's body different from the intellect, which makes something into a human? The question of universals—are substances and accidents only particulars?—was also debated intensely (and it was an important topic in Byzantium, though often considered using late ancient positions).

Aristotelian conceptions were also challenged or rejected. Where Aristotle held that quantity is infinitely divisible, atomism was popular among 12th-century Latin writers and some 14th-century ones. It was also a feature of *kalām*, and the arguments for atomism found there were extensively criticized by Arabic thinkers. Thoroughgoing critiques of the physical basis of Aristotelian metaphysics were made by two (unrelated) Jewish thinkers: al-Baghdādī in the 12th century, and Crescas in the 14th century. The metaphysics of facts and states of affairs, barely hinted at by Aristotle, was explored by Abelard and 14th-century Latin theologians. The Aristotelian view of necessity as what is always true was queried or rejected, most famously by Scotus, but in the Arabic tradition too. The Aristotelian system of causes was taken over, but al-Ghazālī in the Arabic, and Nicholas of Autrecourt (*c*.1298–1369) in the Latin tradition, advanced subtle sceptical arguments about efficient causation.

Time and its relation to eternity was extensively treated by Jewish, Christian, and Arabic thinkers, especially in relation to two theological questions: divine foreknowledge and whether or not the universe had a beginning (as their religions held and Aristotle denied). Christian thinkers were led to elaborate theories about relations, individuation, and wholes and parts, in order to understand the doctrine of the Trinity and the hypostatic union (how divine and human nature combine in the person of Christ).

As indicated, most of these topics were seen as belonging to logic, physics, or theology. 'Metaphysics' in the Middle Ages was restricted to questions directly relating to Aristotle's text of that name. The *Metaphysics* studies 'being in so far as it is being'. Thinkers in Islam and the Latin universities asked whether this means its subject is God, or rather the being which all existing things share. In the Latin tradition, they elaborated a whole theory of transcendentals—attributes such as unity, truth, and goodness, which it was thought all things have simply in virtue of existing. Some Latin writers, such as Albert the Great, thought that the *Book of Causes* completed the *Metaphysics*; and there were some thinkers in each of the traditions who used Platonic notions of Ideas or emanation to shape their theories about being.

Epistemology, philosophy of mind, and philosophy of language

Like the Sceptics in antiquity, and modern philosophers such as Descartes and Hume, medieval philosophers made and answered arguments which cast doubt on our ability to gain knowledge. Augustine's *Against the Academics*, written to refute a sceptical text by Cicero, was an important starting point for 13th- and 14th-century thinkers; but John of Salisbury (1120–80) arrived at his scepticism by reading about the ancient schools. In Byzantium, the sceptical tendencies he found both in Palamas' arguments and those made against him drove Nicholas Cabasilas (d. 1371) to turn to the ancient doxographer, Sextus Empiricus, for sceptical arguments and answers to them. There was a 13th-century Latin translation of Sextus, but in the West he was first used in detail, from the original Greek, by Gianfrancesco Pico della Mirandola (1469–1533), the more famous Giovanni's nephew and editor. Although these sources were not available in Arabic, in his autobiography al-Ghazālī goes through a series of increasingly powerful sceptical arguments similar to those with which Descartes would begin his *Meditations*. More important, though, than answering scepticism was a constructive epistemology,

examining how to build up a structure of scientific knowledge, using the *Posterior Analytics* as a guide and seen as part of logic.

Aristotle's *On Interpretation* encouraged thinking which tied together philosophy of mind and philosophy of language, as seen in al-Fārābī and Abelard (both wrote commentaries on it). In the Latin tradition, the attempt in the 13th century to make grammar an Aristotelian science led to speculative grammar, in which the parallels were drawn between how things are, how they are thought, and how they are expressed in parts of speech and their inflections; while Ockham and Buridan went on to devise sophisticated theories of mental language.

But in all the traditions (though not until after 1200 in the Latin West), it was another of Aristotle's works, *On the Soul*, which was fundamental for investigating perception, memory, and reasoning. Different interpretations of this sometimes enigmatic text supported different theories about how scientific thought and argument is linked to perception and imagination, and to what extent humans can engage in it unaided—theories which meshed with discussions both about the immortality of the soul, and demonstrative science. In their analyses of the process of cognition, both Arabic philosophers and 13th- and 14th-century Latin theologians developed ideas about intentionality which would directly influence the 19th- and 20th-century debate. Another topic explored in detail, especially in the Latin tradition, where Stoic views were pitted against Aristotelian ones, was the nature of emotion.

Ethics and political philosophy

Aristotle's *Nicomachean Ethics* was central to moral philosophy in all four traditions. On the one hand, it encouraged analysis of the virtues and the training of character (in creative tension in the Latin world with the doctrine of theological virtues infused by God into believers). On the other hand, the conclusion in the

final book of the *Ethics*, that the best life for humans is one of intellectual contemplation, proved very attractive to philosophers everywhere, leading them to set out ways to achieve this ideal in this life and so threatening to make the post-mortem salvation promised by Judaism, Christianity, or Islam an irrelevance.

Other currents, however, ran against this happiness-based conception of ethics: for instance, the Mu'tazilites emphasized the demands of morality, not only on humans, but on God, who is duty-bound to reward and punish them; the Ash'arites, and independently, 14th-century Christian theologians like Scotus and Ockham, based morality on divine commands. Through Cicero and Seneca, the Latin tradition also knew about Stoic moral theory, an ethics in which virtue alone is held to be of value. Abelard, who lived before Aristotle's *Ethics* was translated into Latin, devised a moderated Stoic ethics, and Stoic moral ideas continued to be important—for Aquinas, and especially from the 14th century onwards.

Moral psychology became especially developed in the Christian tradition, in part because of the intensive focus on the process of sinning or avoiding sin. Augustine had thought carefully about voluntariness, intention, and culpability, and Anselm about how and why a rational being might choose to do wrong. In the 13th century, Aristotle's treatment of weakness of will complicated this already well developed field.

Arabic and, to a lesser extent, Jewish philosophers were inspired by accounts of Plato's *Republic* and *Laws* to think about the ideal city, which he and they pictured (most implausibly) as governed by philosophers. This type of speculation was absent from the Christian traditions, and among Latin thinkers Aristotle's *Politics* was used as the basis for a more sober study of what form of governance would best promote peace and stability (see Chapter 9).

Philosophy of religion

Philosophy of religion includes both natural theology, which asks, according to reason, about the existence and attributes of a supreme being, and philosophical questioning about the practice of religion: what it involves (faith, worship, sacrifice, and so on) and what is its relation to other forms of knowledge, philosophy included. Both aspects of the subject were studied in all four traditions.

In Arabic, Jewish, and Latin Christian thought, much energy was given to proving the existence of God. Anselm argued that the very notion of God as that than which nothing greater can be conceived shows that God exists, because were that than which nothing greater can be conceived to exist only in conception and not reality, it would be less great than if it existed in reality too, and then it would not be that than which nothing greater can be conceived. Most Latin thinkers, however, followed Aristotle and Avicenna, putting forward 'cosmological' arguments, which do not rely just on a description of God but on some basic feature of the universe. Aquinas' 'five ways' are the most famous, but it was Scotus who provided the most careful and elaborate set of reasoning.

There was intense interest everywhere in the problem of reconciling divine omniscience with human freedom, and the even more difficult problem of showing how God's providence is compatible, not only with human free will, but also with the existence and extent of evil. God's omnipotence also generated questions: how is it related to his goodness, and to his will? Independently, al-Ghazālī and Abelard (and through him the scholastic tradition) asked whether, since he always wills the best, and is able to bring about what he wills, God can do other than he does.

The ways in which God can be spoken about in human language were explored through different schemes of negative theology or

opposition to it (pseudo-Dionysius, Maximus, and Eriugena; Maimonides, Aquinas, and Gersonides; Eckhart); and through considering the names of God (al-Ghazālī), or the relation between God and Aristotle's ten categories (Augustine, Boethius, Eriugena, Gilbert of Poitiers). The relation between scientific knowledge and religious truths was explored from many angles: compare, for instance, Averroes' argument in his *Decisive Treatise* that Muslims capable of it are *obliged* to study Aristotelian philosophy, Aquinas' explanation of why Aristotelian metaphysics does not make Christian theology unnecessary, Maimonides' *Guide* (entire) and the complex explanations put forward by Arts Masters from the 13th to the 16th century, designed to preserve a relative value for the Aristotelian truths they defended while acknowledging that, according to the ultimate arbiter—Christian doctrine—they are falsehoods.

Various writers—for instance, al-Fārābī and Roger Bacon (1214–94), a brilliant Arts Master and then a maverick theologian—also thought about the relations between philosophy and religion by considering their origins. The 14th-century Paris and Oxford theologians were especially keen to investigate the nature of belief and its voluntariness, while an interest in paganism (prominent in Maimonides, for example) helped to give an edge to these enquiries into the nature of religion.

Chapter 5
Institutions and literary forms

In the Middle Ages just as today, philosophers were not disembodied intellects (much as some of them wanted, or want, to be). They had to do their work in a concrete setting, within or outside an institution, and support themselves, either as professional scholars and teachers or in some other way. And their thinking has been preserved only in so far as it has been given concrete existence in literary texts in a variety of forms, some of which give an idea of the type of teaching and discussion behind them.

Philosophy outside and inside institutions

Institutionally, the history of Latin Christian philosophy is strikingly different from that of the other three traditions, because so much of the best work took place in—and, especially after 1200, was shaped by—institutions dedicated to teaching and learning.

The contrast is not an absolute one. There was, sporadically, some type of Imperial institution of higher education at Constantinople. It was presumably where the mysterious Stephanus, from the School of Alexandria, taught at the beginning of the 7th century. In the mid-9th century, the Assistant Emperor Bardas established a school at the Magnaura Palace there, but it seems not to have lasted long. A school was set up in the 11th century for Psellos,

who was given the title 'Consul of the Philosophers', but after the condemnation of his pupil and successor, Italos, the Patriarchate was increasingly responsible for a higher education which had little room for philosophy. Many of the important Byzantine philosophers were monks—Maximus, John of Damascus, Gregory Palamas—or court politicians who became monks, such as Photius (tonsured and promoted to be Patriarch of Constantinople in just five days) and Psellus.

In Islamic lands, the focus of teaching and learning was never institutional: rather, it was on the relationship between teacher and pupil. When a student had properly studied a text under a master, he received an *izāl*, or licence, which allowed him, in his turn, to teach it. Great store was placed, as the example of al-Fārābī has already shown, on being able to trace a chain of teachers back to the author of the text in question himself. Where the instruction took place mattered for little.

No institutions existed specially for studying philosophy (either *kalām* or *falsafa*). Al-Kindī was a nobleman, able to support his own and others' work. Avicenna, like al-Ṭūsī two centuries later, led a stormy life, swayed by the fortunes of the rulers who were his patrons. Avicenna was a physician, no less celebrated as a medical author than as a philosopher (and many of his early readers were also physicians); al-Ṭūsī was famous as an astronomer, and ended his life as a vizier. Al-Ghazālī was a distinguished teacher of law, until he renounced worldly fortune. Averroes was a doctor, as well as a renowned lawyer, whose legal writing continued to be studied in the lands of Islam, where his philosophy was forgotten; he wrote his Aristotelian commentaries at night, while in the daytime he served as chief judge.

Islam was not, however, without higher educational institutions. *Madrasas*, intended for the teaching of law, could be set up by benefactors, and their numbers expanded from the late 12th century. This was also the period when not only did the

distinction between *falsafa* and *kalām* begin to disappear but also what had previously been seen as 'foreign sciences' started to be placed along with more specifically Islamic subjects under the heading of 'rational sciences', which came to be thought of as part of a broad Muslim education. The study of this broad curriculum was certainly associated with *madrasas* and their teachers, although it is difficult to be sure about exactly where the teaching of any particular subject was conducted.

Among the Jews too there were no official institutions for philosophy. Family wealth seems to have supported Gersonides, and Maimonides, too, until his merchant brother was drowned and he had to support himself as a physician to the Cairo court. Many of the outstanding Jewish philosophers were also central figures in the Jewish life of their times. Maimonides was the chief of the Egyptian Jewish community and their greatest expert on Jewish law; Saadia was the head (Gaon) of the Talmudic Academy; Crescas the leader of the Spanish Jews; Isaac Abrabanel an influential figure in court, who tried, unsuccessfully, to use his wealth and prestige to dissuade King Ferdinand from banishing the Jews.

The universities and other settings for Latin philosophy

The earliest philosophers in the Latin tradition, Alcuin and Eriugena, were each closely associated with the Carolingian court, but as teachers at a palace school. They also had close connections with monasteries, and it was in schools established in the great monasteries, and then also in cathedral schools, that philosophy was studied in the 10th and 11th centuries. Cathedral schools seemed each to have had just one main Master, who was able, like Abelard's teacher, William of Champeaux, to draw pupils from far off if he became celebrated. But, early in the 12th century, the authorities at Notre-Dame in Paris decided that they would allow any qualified teacher, who paid for a licence, to set up a school. As

a result, Paris became the intellectual capital of the Latin world, with Masters competing for pupils and developing their own ideas, as they attacked those of their neighbouring rivals.

Universities specializing in law (Bologna) or medicine (Salerno) already existed in southern Europe, but it was only around 1200 that the medieval universities which would be especially important for philosophy came into existence: in Paris from a formalization of the existing schools, in Oxford from almost nothing. From the mid-14th century, universities on the Paris–Oxford model began to be founded all over Europe. Among the first were Prague (1347–78), Krakow (1364), Vienna (1365), and Heidelberg (1386); 15th-century foundations included St Andrew's, Louvain, Tübingen, and Alcalá.

The distinction in the logical and theological schools in Paris became institutionalized into a structure of faculties, followed with some variations in all the universities north of the Alps. The Arts Faculty, by far the largest, was where students began (at around the age of fourteen). Most did not even finish the full seven-year course. But after becoming a Master of Arts, students who wished could go on to study in one of the higher faculties—medicine, law, or (by far the most important for philosophy) theology. Logic was studied intently in the Arts Faculty, but from the mid-13th century the arts curriculum covered not just Aristotle's logic, but the whole range of his works, newly translated (with Avicenna and Averroes as the favoured guides). The theology course, which lasted for between fourteen and sixteen years, had just two textbooks, the Bible and the *Sentences* of Peter the Lombard, which acted like a checklist of the whole range of difficult and controversial issues in Christian doctrine.

The universities were institutions under the ultimate control of the Church, and two of their higher faculties (theology and canon law) were explicitly devoted to Christian doctrine. Very quickly,

the Dominicans, Franciscans, and other mendicant orders dominated the theology faculties. These orders, which grew up at much the same time as the universities themselves, offered a life which was monastic but not shut away from the world. In practice, they made it possible for bright boys, whatever their background, to be educated to a high level and, for the most able of them, they paid the expenses of the lengthy theology course. At the end of the course, the student became a Master, but there was a limited number of magisterial chairs, and so, after a couple of years, the Dominican and Franciscan Masters had to stand aside for the next confrere in line.

Although these mendicant Masters had been highly trained in logic and Aristotelian philosophy, it was in their own houses of study, not in the faculties of Arts. Many of those who taught in the Arts Faculty would have been young men spending the two years for which they were required to teach in order to complete their course. But there were others, such as Buridan, who dedicated themselves to teaching in the Arts Faculty. There all the disciplines were based on evidence available irrespective of religious belief and natural reasoning, and the greatest authority, around whose texts the course was structured, was a pagan from the ancient, pre-Christian world.

This arrangement might seem to represent a challenge to the authority of Christian teaching, but in fact was sanctioned, even enforced, by the Church authorities. True, when the whole range of Aristotle's works, including those on natural science and the *Metaphysics*, began to be read in the early 13th century, the Church authorities in Paris tried to stop Arts Masters teaching them. But the prohibitions were ineffective, and it was quickly accepted that the Arts course would be based around the whole Aristotelian corpus. There remained, however, questions about the degree of allegiance Arts Masters should show to Aristotelianism, especially as interpreted in the commentaries by writers from Islam.

In 1277, Étienne Tempier, Bishop of Paris, issued a list of 219 prohibited propositions. Some of the prohibitions were clearly directed at Arts Masters like Siger of Brabant and Boethius of Dacia, whose attempts to develop Aristotelianism in its own terms were caricatured and condemned. But they were not Tempier's only target, since he also prohibited various positions in theology, especially those judged to compromise the freedom of God and his particular providence for humans, and—as a later, aborted process of condemnation indicates—Aquinas' Aristotelianism was also in his sights.

A culture of commentaries

One common feature distinguishes how philosophy was studied and written about in all four traditions from modern and contemporary practice. Medieval philosophizing centred around commentary, a method inherited from the late ancient Platonic schools, but widespread generally in the medieval monotheistic cultures (consider the practice of Biblical and Quranic commentary) and beyond (Confucianism, for instance, is a commentary tradition).

Aristotle's works, of course, were much commented on, throughout the Byzantine and Latin traditions, and in the first two centuries of *falsafa* (see Figure 6); Plato's much more rarely (the *Timaeus* in the pre-1200 Latin tradition, Averroes on an epitome of the *Republic*); Platonic writings more often (Boethius' *Consolation of Philosophy*, the *Book of Causes*, Proclus' *Elements of Theology* in the Latin traditions). It was not just ancient texts which were the subject of commentaries. The Hebrew-writing Jewish philosophers usually commented on Averroes' paraphrases of Aristotle rather than Aristotle himself, and on texts by, for example, Maimonides, al-Ghazālī, Ibn Ṭufayl, and Averroes (see Figure 7). In the Arabic tradition, there was always a tendency for new encyclopaedic works, based on earlier ones, and for commentaries themselves, to receive commentaries. Aristotle's

6. The paraphrase of Aristotle's *Categories* misattributed to Augustine was one of the earliest logical texts to receive commentary, as here in the margins of a 9th-century manuscript.

own texts dropped almost completely out of the picture, although Avicenna's works continued to receive direct commentaries, alongside the commentaries written on work deriving (ultimately) from them.

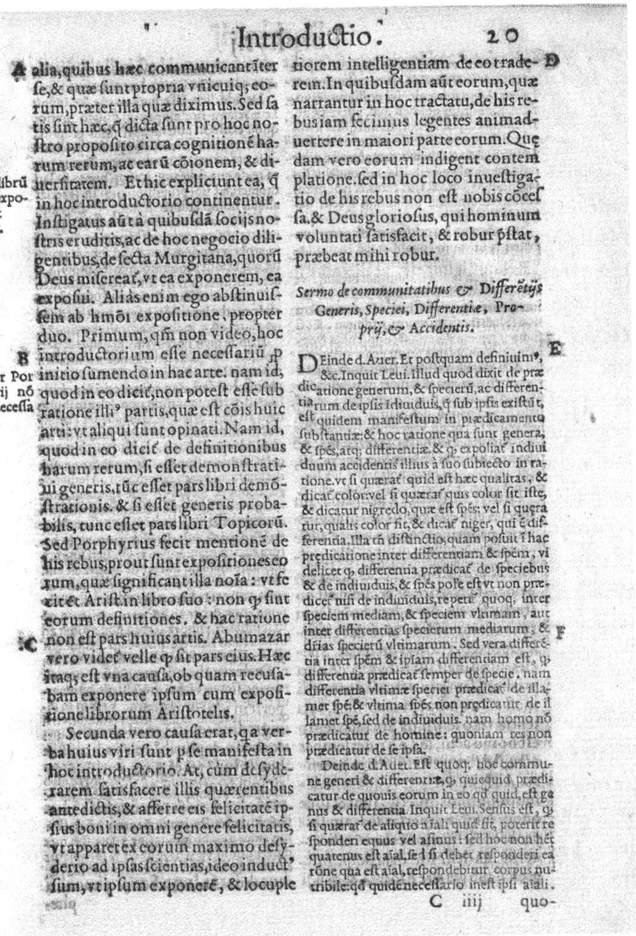

Introductio. 20

A alia, quibus hæc communicant iter se, & quæ sunt propria vnicuiq; eorum, præter illa quæ diximus. Sed satis sint hæc, q̄ dicta sunt pro hoc nostro proposito circa cognitionē harum rerum, ac earū cōionem, & diuersitatem. Et hic expliciunt ea, q̄ in hoc introductorio continentur. Instigatus aūt à quibusdā socijs nostris eruditis, ac de hoc negocio diligentibus, de secta Murgitana, quorū Deus misereat, vt ea exponerem, ea exposui. Aliàs enim ego abstinuissem ab hmōi expositione, propter duo. Primum, qm̄ non video, hoc B introductorium esse necessariū ꝓ initio sumendo in hac arte. nam id, quod in eo dicit, non potest esse sub ratione illi⁹ partis, quæ est cōis huic arti: vt aliqui sunt opinati. Nam id, quod in eo dicit de definitionibus harum rerum, si esset demonstratiui generis, tūc esset pars libri demōstrationis. & si esset generis probabilis, tunc esset pars libri Topicorū. Sed Porphyrius fecit mentionē de his rebus, prout sunt expositiones eorum, quæ significant illa noīa: vt fecit et Arist. in libro suo: non q̄ sint eorum definitiones. & hac ratione C non est pars huius artis. Abumazar vero videt velle q̄ sit pars eius. Hæc itaq; est vna causa, ob quam recusabam exponere ipsum cum expositione librorum Aristotelis.

Secunda vero causa erat, q a verba huius viri sunt ꝑ se manifesta in hoc introductorio. At, cùm desyderarem satisfacere illis quærentibus antedictis, & afferre eis felicitatē ipsius boni in omni genere felicitatis, vt apparet ex eorum maximo desyderio ad ipsas scientias, ideo induct⁹ sum, vt ipsum exponerē, & locuple

Cur librū hūc exposuerit Auer.

Liber Porphyrij nō est necessarius.

D tiorem intelligentiam de eo tradere. In quibusdam aūt eorum, quæ narrantur in hoc tractatu, de his rebus iam fecimus legentes animaduertere in maiori parte eorum. Quędam vero eorum indigent contemplatione. sed in hoc loco inuestigatio de his rebus non est nobis cōcessa. & Deus gloriosus, qui hominum voluntati satisfacit, & robur ꝑstat, præbeat mihi robur.

Sermo de communitatibus & Differētijs Generis, Speciei, Differentiæ, Proprij, & Accidentis.

E Deinde d. Auer. Et postquam definiuim⁹, &c. Inquit Leui. Illud quod dixit de prædicatione generum, & specierū, ac differentiarum de ipsis indiuiduis, q̄ sub ipsis existūt, est quidem manifestum in prædicamento substantiæ: & hoc ratione qua sunt genera, & spēs, atq; differentiæ, & q̄ expoliat indiuiduum accidentis illius à suo subiecto in ratione. vt si quærat quid est hæc qualitas, & dicat color: vel si quærat quis color sit iste, & dicatur nigredo, quæ est spēs: vel si quęratur, qualis color sit, & dicat niger, qui ē differentia. Illa tñ distinctio, quam posuit ī hac prędicatione inter differentiam & spēm, videlicet q̄ differentia prædicat de speciebus & de indiuiduis, & spēs pot̄e est vt non prædicet nisi de indiuiduis, reperit quoq; inter speciem mediam, & speciem vltimam, aut F inter differentias specierum mediarum, & drīas specierū vltimarum. Sed vera differētia inter spēm & ipsam differentiam est, q̄ differentia prædicat semper de specie. nam differentia vltimæ speciei prædicat de illamet spē: & vltima spēs non prędicat de illamet spē, sed de indiuiduis. nam homo nō prædicatur de homine: quoniam res non prædicatur de se ipsa.

Deinde d. Auer. Est quoq; hoc commune generi & differentiæ, q̄ quicquid prædicatur de quouis eorum in eo qd̄ quid, est genus & differentia. Inquit Leui. Sensus est, q̄ si quærat de aliquo aīali quid sit, poterit responderi equus vel asinus: sed hoc non hēt quatenus est aīal, sed si debet responderi ea rōne qua est aīal, respondebitur corpus nutribile: qd̄ quidē necessario inest ipsi aīali.

C iiij quo-

7. Aristotle with Averroes' commentaries and Gersonides' super-commentaries, all in Latin translation, from a mid-16th-century edition.

In the Latin tradition, a 12th-century work (though heavily based on Augustine), the *Sentences* of Peter the Lombard, was commented on by hundreds of theologians, from Alexander of Hales in the 13th century to Martin Luther in the 16th century.

And, from the 16th century, Aquinas' *Summa Theologiae* received regular commentaries, and Scotists commented on their founder's *Sentences* commentary.

Commentaries varied enormously in their methods and aims. Some were designed mainly to help with understanding a difficult authoritative text, either by explaining each sentence and its contribution to the argument (for example, the literal element in the commentaries on Aristotle in the Latin tradition in the 12th and 13th centuries) or through paraphrase (one of the forms used by al-Fārābī and Averroes). Some discuss the interpretation of the text passage by passage, exploring the philosophical difficulties and putting forward new problems and theories, suggested by, but not actually found in the original work. Many late ancient commentaries were in this form, which Boethius followed in his second commentary on *On Interpretation*, Abelard in his logical commentaries and al-Fārābī and Averroes in their long commentaries. Avicenna's encyclopaedic presentations of his own rethinking of Aristotelian doctrine are to some extent paraphrase commentaries, although loose ones. Albert the Great imitated this form.

Commentary on some texts (Plato's *Timaeus* and Boethius' *Consolation of Philosophy* in the 12th century, for instance) called at times for allegorical exegesis, like that used for sacred texts. The relation of commentator to text was often one of reverence (as with Averroes and Latin Arts Masters towards Aristotle)—though this did not in fact exclude original thinking. But it could be antagonistic, as with al-Rāzī's commentary on *Pointers* or in the case of Albalag, who deliberately chose to comment on al-Ghazālī's *Intentions*, though he disliked both the Avicennian philosophy it summarized and, even more, al-Ghazālī's wider, anti-philosophical aims. A more historical approach to a text, in terms of its author's aims and sources, was rare, but is carried through with remarkable perspicacity by Aquinas in his commentary on the *Book of Causes*.

The quaestio

Many Latin commentaries from 1250 onwards owe their freedom to raise new ideas to their use of the *quaestio* form, a feature of most Aristotle and *Sentence* commentaries (with Albert and Aquinas on Aristotle as important exceptions), even if they also include a literal element. (Interestingly, a form similar to the *quaestio* began to be used in Arabic philosophy at much the same time—for instance, in the work of al-Rāzī.) Although aspects of the *quaestio* are found in Aristotle and Boethius, the form seems to have been devised principally as a way of capturing the give and take of discussion in university lectures—particularly evident in the disputations which were held on special days, but also a feature of how authoritative texts were taught.

A *quaestio* has as its subject a 'yes' or 'no' question: for instance, 'Does God exist?' It takes the following basic form:

1. 'It seems that God does not exist.' Arguments (1...n) will then be given for this view (which is always either the opposite of the view the author actually holds, or at least will be rejected by him as not true without qualification).
2. 'But against this.' A short statement, usually from authority, will be given for the opposite view (i.e. here, that God exists).
3. The body of the *quaestio*. Here the writer will go into the matter at issue and argue for his own view of the question. (In this example, the writer would advance arguments to show that God does exist.)
4. Each of the arguments (1...n) for the opposite of the writer's view is considered and rejected, often on the basis of the positions established in (3).

Although this form could be used for fairly straightforward exegesis, as it often was in Arts Faculty Aristotle commentaries (here the arguments in (1) will be obvious misreadings of the text,

and the body (3) will expound Aristotle's point), it also offered great opportunities to develop new ideas, using the arguments in (1) to test out objections and bring in a range of authorities beyond the text actually being commented upon. In the case of *Sentence* commentaries, indeed, Peter the Lombard's text was usually left far behind, as theologians used one of the points it raised to discuss the burning philosophical issues of the time, and the body (3) was often expanded into an independent philosophical essay, with its own divisions and subdivisions.

Summas and treatises

In all four traditions, there was also a tendency for thinkers to try to bring together in a single work their understanding of the whole of philosophy or theology. In Arabic philosophy, the tradition of philosophical encyclopaedias developed out of Avicenna's way of commenting on Aristotle, while the theological *summas* had a long tradition in *kalām*. John of Damascus's *On the Orthodox Faith*, translated into Latin, was one of the models for the theological *summas* popular in the 13th century. The best known of them all, Aquinas' *Summa Theologiae*, was an attempt to bring university-level discussion to a broader range of students at Dominican houses of study, although it turned out to be not just a summary of views its author had developed elsewhere, but his fullest discussion of some fields, such as ethics. Among Jewish authors—from Ibn Daud in *The Exalted Faith* and Maimonides in his *Guide of the Perplexed* to Gersonides' *Wars of the Lord* and the monumental *Light of the Lord* by Crescas—there was a tradition of writing a lengthy philosophical and theological treatise which aimed to cover all the problems the author thought most important.

Of course, shorter forms of philosophical writing were also used, and treatises were written about individual issues, sometimes as part of a controversy, sometimes as letters to a real or fictitious correspondent. Many of al-Kindī's works take the form of letters;

Ibn Bājja wrote a letter on conjunction with the Intellect, Eriugena wrote on predestination in order to attack the views of his contemporary, Gottschalk, and Maimonides wrote to defend his views about the resurrection of the dead. In the Latin universities there were disputations, written up in *quaestio* form, both on particular areas (the soul, power, evil) and so-called disputations *de quolibet* ('about anything'), where a student was free to raise any problem of philosophical or theological interest.

Dialogues and other literary forms

Even where medieval philosophers do not base their writings directly on their teaching, they usually aim to put their ideas in a straightforward, if sometimes complex, way, without rhetoric or the use of a literary form which deliberately raises problems of interpretation: they are more like Aristotle, Kant, and today's analytic philosophers than Plato, Kierkegaard, or Heidegger. But there are exceptions.

Versification was used in both Arabic and Latin as a way of making material easier to learn by heart, and sometimes literary form was used more adventurously. Ibn Ṭufayl expresses his thought in the form of a philosophical novel, taking the names of his characters from one of Avicenna's ventures into explaining philosophical ideas in allegorical form. Maimonides warns readers of his *Guide* that he has deliberately obscured some of his ideas. Boethius' much read *Consolation* is an elaborate literary construction, in prose and verse. In 12th-century Latin Europe, philosophical poems and prose and verse works (such as Bernard Silvestris' *Cosmographia*, loosely based on the *Timaeus*) were popular, and Dante's *Divine Comedy* is not just a great poem but also an original and powerful work of philosophy.

Dialogue form was a popular vehicle for philosophy in Byzantium—where it could imitate Plato or take a satirical turn with Lucian as a model—and, even more, in the early Latin

tradition. There the dialogue was often didactic: Alcuin, for example, presented himself as a teacher with Charlemagne himself as his pupil; Eriugena's *Periphyseon* presents the give and take of discussion between a Master and his alumnus; and Anselm makes his dialogues into models of sensitive instruction in philosophical method (while his *Proslogion* is a dialogue between himself and God).

In the 15th century, under the influence of humanism, the form again became popular—in the works of Nicholas of Cusa, for example, or Lorenzo Valla's Ciceronian dialogue *On Pleasure*. Some dialogues explored the differences between religions. In his *Kuzari*, Judah Halevi (*c*.1075–1141) has a philosopher, a Christian, and a Muslim present their beliefs briefly, although most of the work is occupied by a Jewish sage, who offers a more convincing view. Halevi's Latin contemporary, Peter Abelard, is less eager to champion his own religion in his *Collationes*, where a philosopher discourses with a Jew (who gives a remarkably Abelardian version of his faith) and a Christian, with whom he finds much to agree about the highest good. The *Dialogue of the Gentile and the Three Sages* by Ramon Llull is even more open. When the Gentile of the title has heard expositions of Judaism, Christianity, and Islam from each of the sages, he is ready to tell them which has convinced him, but they stop him, fearing that knowledge of his verdict might put an end to their own continuing conversations.

Chapter 6
Universals (Avicenna and Abelard)

There is a core question about universals, which perplexed ancient and medieval thinkers, and still exercises philosophers today; they have even borrowed the medieval nomenclature for the main positions taken. Some things in the world are the same, not by being numerically identical (as John Marenbon is numerically identical with the author of this book), but by being the same in some respect: this saucer, that coin, and that mirror are all the same, for instance, in being round; all the animals in that field are the same in being horses. Is it enough simply to suppose that there are these many particular things which are the same in these respects, or is there some additional entity, besides the particular things—a universal—in respect of which they are the same? Those who believe there are such entities—universal things—are called 'realists'; those who consider that real universals are unnecessary are 'nominalists' (from the Latin *nomen* = name): they accept that there are universals in language (such as the words 'round' and 'horse'), but deny that there are universal things.

There is at least one striking difference between medieval and contemporary ways of posing the 'problem of universals'. It is partly, but not wholly, a matter of terminology. In the *Categories*, Aristotle divides things into substances and nine sorts of accident (see Chapter 4). A primary substance is a particular belonging to a natural kind, not the result of human artifice: a man or woman, a

flower or a stone (but not a table or a house). The accidents are properties which attach to substances, and can come and go. So, for example, 'Fat red-faced John, Arthur's son, is sitting, wearing a jacket, in the kitchen this morning, eating and hearing the music' describes a primary substance, John, and his accidents in each of the categories. John also has properties, known as *differentiae*, which are not accidents because he cannot be without them: they include rationality, a defining feature of all humans, and having sense perception, a defining feature of all animals, human and non-human. In the Middle Ages, the problem of universals was usually posed about substances.

Medieval thinkers asked whether, in addition to the primary substances, there are universal secondary substances: species (such as Man), and genera (such as Animal or Living Thing) which bring together different species. Philosophers today not only use a different terminology; they also usually discuss universal properties, such as roundness or redness, rather than substances. One reason for the difference is a gap between medieval and contemporary science. Following Aristotle, most medieval thinkers thought of natural kinds as fixed and determinate, whereas we consider them to be continuously evolving and to have fuzzy boundaries. This difference is not, however, as wide as it first appears. Medieval writers did also discuss universal properties (accidents and *differentiae*, in their terms), and many contemporary philosophers accept that there are some determinate, fixed natural kinds, such as water, and these do indeed figure in some contemporary discussions about universals.

The problem of universals in antiquity

Notoriously, Plato held that there are really existent independent Ideas or Forms which alone truly exist and are the objects of knowledge. These Ideas filled the role of universals, although Plato conceived them rather as particulars which served as

paradigms for all other particulars. Aristotle rejected Platonic Ideas, but, according to most interpretations, he was a realist who denied that universals exist independently of or outside the particulars which instantiate them, except in the mind. Alexander of Aphrodisias, the greatest of the ancient followers of Aristotle, who died early in the 3rd century AD, developed Aristotle's position by tackling a serious problem it faces. Alexander argues that an Aristotelian universal must in some way be in its particulars. But universals are not divided out between particulars as parts, in the way we might share a cake—as if this horse had part of the universal Horse and that horse another part. Every horse is wholly a horse: the universal is entire within each of its many particulars. But, Alexander points out, no thing can be wholly in many numerically different particulars. Suppose that the whole universal Horse were in Black Beauty, then it could not be in any other thing, and so the only horse would be Black Beauty. Universals, therefore, cannot be things, and so they must just be mental conceptions. If so, however, they must be empty, misleading conceptions, since it has just been admitted that nothing in reality corresponds to them.

Alexander answers the objection by turning to the idea of abstraction. In geometry, for instance, we conceive figures, such as squares and triangles, apart from matter, although they can exist only in matter. But we do not regard these conceptions as empty or misleading. Alexander applied the same reasoning to universals. But the path he suggests is not straightforward. If the solution is to remain a realist one, it has to explain how there is a basis in reality for the universal concept abstracted in the mind, and yet avoid making that basis into a thing wholly within many numerically different particulars.

Avicenna on universals

One of the most sophisticated and influential ways of dealing with this problem was proposed by Avicenna, probably basing himself

on some of Alexander's ideas. Consider an act of abstraction. Suppose we want to think about horses, abstracting from all the accidental features of this or that horse, such as its white or chestnut colour, and just considering what it is in virtue of which they are horses: what Avicenna calls, apparently interchangeably, 'horse in as much as it is horse' or 'horseness in as much as it is horseness'.

According to our usual way of thinking about abstraction, we would distinguish two elements: the real horses, such as Black Beauty and Bucephalus, which are particular things, and our abstracted mental conception of Horse or horseness, which is a universal, since it relates to every particular horse. Avicenna, however, understands that abstraction can be seen not just in terms of its result—a mental conception—but in terms of what it picks out in reality, as the basis for the mental conception. When I am abstracting, then I am regarding Black Beauty simply in as much it is a horse: I am picking out what Avicenna sometimes calls a 'nature'—in this case, horse(ness)—and basing my mental conception on it. And so there are in fact three elements: horse(ness) in as much as it is horse(ness)—the nature; the particular thing—Black Beauty; and the mental conception of horse(ness). The nature, horse(ness), Avicenna insists is in itself absolutely nothing except horse(ness). By contrast, the particular thing consists, not just of horse(ness), but also of all the accidents that characterize Black Beauty. The mental conception of horseness adds universality to the nature on which it is based, which in itself is neither universal nor particular.

Avicenna's position, it might at first sight seem, could be summarized as being that there are natures, particular real things, and universal concepts. Natures themselves are neither particular nor universal, but become particular real things when accidents are added to them, and, when conceived in the mind, have universality added to them and become universal concepts.

Avicenna's view was, indeed, taken in this way by some of his medieval Latin readers, but he would have rejected this way of treating natures as some special sort of thing. The immediate question, Avicenna realizes, which a critic will put to him about his notion of nature is whether the horse(ness) in Black Beauty is different from the horse(ness) in Bucephalus. If he says 'Yes', then how will he maintain that they are both horses? If he denies it, then it will follow that numerically one horse(ness) is in both, and so numerically the same thing is wholly in numerically different particulars.

Avicenna takes the only way out: he denies both that the horse(ness) in Black Beauty is different from the horse(ness) in Bucephalus and that the two horse(nesse)s are numerically one. Since he accepts that to be different is simply not to be numerically one, he seems to be denying the principle of the excluded middle (that for any x and any F, x either is F or is not F). But Avicenna avoids doing so by insisting that we should refuse to answer the question 'Is horse(ness) in as much as it is horse(ness) one or not one?' It is a malformed question, because it takes horse(ness) in as much as it is horse(ness) as if it were some sort of thing, a nature, which is a subject for predication (that is to say, something about which we can say 'It is one', 'It is not one', as we say that this page is white).

The horseness in Black Beauty is neither different from that in Bucephalus, nor the same in number as it. When we consider horseness in as much as it is horseness, Avicenna holds, we are simply understanding Black Beauty or Bucephalus in a special way, which disregards many features which no particular horse can be without. Horseness in as much as it is horseness is not another thing, over and beyond the particular horses, about which problems concerning whether it is one or many can arise, but it does provide a basis in reality for the universal concept of horse we can form in our minds.

Early medieval realism

Alexander of Aphrodisias' argument against the existence of universals was made known to philosophers in the Latin tradition by Boethius. Boethius also proposed a version of Alexander's abstractionist response, but in a rather unclear way which left room for philosophers in the schools of the early 12th century to propose various, conflicting Boethian answers to the problem of universals. The abstracted universal concepts in the mind were unproblematic, but the 12th-century thinkers struggled to explain how they were based on real universals in particulars: what did Boethius mean by saying that the same likeness (for example, the likeness of horse) is both something that can be perceived by the senses in particulars and yet is grasped by the intellect alone as a universal?

One interpretation, 'material essence realism' (MER), was popular in the early 1100s and reflects an approach that was common before thinkers began to study Boethius' solution closely. According to MER, universals underlie particulars as their material. Black Beauty is, then, the universal, Horse, which is individuated—that is to say, made into this particular horse—by its accidents, such as his black colour, his size, weight, and position in place and time; Bucephalus is exactly the same universal, Horse, but with different individuating accidents.

MER has, then, a strongly realist conception of universals. According to it, Aristotle's primary substances are simply the one secondary substance together with individuating accidents. Other interpreters of Boethius avoided holding that there are underlying, material-like universal substances. Instead, they proposed that Black Beauty and Bucephalus are simply 'not different' from each other in respect of being horses, and the universal Horse has its basis in the collection of all horses, and also—some held—in the individual horses in so far as they are horses. Some of these theorists would, therefore, claim that

everything is a particular. But they remained realists, since they held that universals exist too, as collections of particulars or even as the particulars themselves.

Abelard on universals

Abelard argued powerfully against all these versions of realism. He pointed out that it was incoherent to hold, as MER does, that accidents individuate substances. Accidents are dependent on their substances: if there were no Black Beauty, his blackness would not exist. But if Black Beauty is individuated by his accidents, then his blackness and other accidents need to exist in order for Black Beauty to exist. Moreover, Abelard claims that, since according to MER it is the same universal animal which exists in John Marenbon and Black Beauty, it will have to be at once both rational and irrational, which is impossible. Against the collection theory he objected that collections are unlike universals because they are not in all their members as a whole, and they come after and consist of their members.

Abelard's most striking contribution to the history of the problem of universals lies, however, not in these arguments against realist theories but in the conclusion he drew from them. Unlike any of his predecessors, he did not try to devise a more subtle realist position, or openly invoke the idea of common natures, but insisted that universals are just words. He was the first to defend this nominalist position (and, indeed, the word 'nominalist' was first coined to describe him and his followers).

True, one of his teachers, Roscelin of Compiègne, anticipated Abelard's position in some respects. In the early 1090s, Anselm attacked Roscelin for holding that universals are nothing more than the breath emitted when a word is uttered. Roscelin and a few of his contemporaries apparently believed that logic is concerned exclusively with language, and that the various special

terms used by logicians—not just 'universals', but also '*differentiae*' and 'accidents'—therefore signify other words, not things. But none of them tried to provide, as Abelard would do, the central element of a nominalist theory of universals: an account of how we can talk about the world using universal words (as we do when we say 'Black Beauty is a horse' or 'Horses are animals'), if there are no universal things.

Abelard sees language as related to the world in two main ways. Words 'nominate', that is to say refer to, things in the world, and they also 'signify' things, by producing a concept of them in the hearer's mind. Abelard recognizes that there are problems about both sorts of semantic relationship, if he wants to hold that there no real universals. But he believes they can be overcome. Universal words cannot nominate universal things, because there are *no* universal things, but they can nominate all the particulars which fall under them: so 'man' nominates John, Joan, Jan, and every other human. Abelard recognizes, however, that a universal word like 'man' does not nominate John in the same way that 'John' does. 'John' nominates John as a discrete individual. 'Man' nominates John according to how he comes together with other humans, to his nature as a human being.

It is this coming together which, according to Abelard, is the 'common cause of imposition' of the universal word 'man'. And, of course, Abelard strenuously denies that being a man (or, as he also calls it, the *status* of man) is a thing of any sort. Particular men, he says, 'come together in this, that they are men'. And he then adds: 'I do not say "in man"—since nothing is man other than a discrete thing—but in being a man. Being a man is neither man nor any thing, if we consider it carefully.'

The most difficult problem for interpreters of Abelard's theory is to know precisely what position he is taking here. On one view, he is like a 21st-century austere nominalist, who simply declares that things fall into various groups by being similar to each other in a

certain respect and that such similarity needs no further explanation. On another view, although Abelard is able to say that *status* are not things because they are not substances or accidents, the only two sorts of thing his Aristotle-based ontology admits, they do in fact play the role of things—they are close to Avicennian natures—and allow him to give a realistic twist to his theory, despite his claims to have rejected realism.

Abelard's problem about the other semantic relationship, the signification of thoughts, is that, if there are no universal things, then there is no object of which a universal word can produce a thought. This objection gains its force from his way of answering the first one: if 'man' is imposed from a common cause, then this community of cause prevents it from producing the thought of any one human being. Abelard replies by explaining how we can create all sorts of conceptions or images in our mind, among them conceptions which are not of one particular but are common to many particulars of the same sort. So, for instance, I can create an image of something which is neither John, Joan, nor Jan, but just an image of a human being: it is this 'common conception' which is the object of thought when I hear the word 'man'.

Duns Scotus: transforming Avicenna's solution

Although Abelard had many followers in the second half of the 12th century, with the arrival of new Aristotelian and Arabic sources his nominalism was forgotten. Avicenna's treatment of universals was very influential, but interpreted in various ways. Duns Scotus took over Avicenna's idea that the nature of something can be considered just in itself, but he adapted it. The central problem for Avicenna's theory is to explain how horse(ness) in as much it is horse(ness) is neither numerically one (because in that case one thing would be wholly present in many) nor diverse in number (because in that case it would not explain how both Black Beauty and Bucephalus are horses). Avicenna

himself argues that it is numerically neither one nor diverse, because it is nothing except horseness, and so it is not some sort of thing to which being one or not being one can be attributed. Scotus proposes, rather, that horseness is numerically neither one nor diverse because it is one, but not *numerically* one. Unlike Avicenna, then, Scotus is willing to treat a common nature as a thing, but it is a sort of thing which, he says, has, not numerical unity, but 'less-than-numerical unity'.

There are for Scotus, therefore, two sorts of unity: numerical unity or singularity, by which Black Beauty is one thing and Bucephalus another; and the less-than-numerical unity which their common nature, horseness, has in virtue of its being the same horseness, though in many numerically diverse horses. Precisely because horseness is *less-than*-numerically unified, it can be wholly in many numerically different things while still being (in some way) one.

But why accept that anything can be unified in this less-than-numerical way? Scotus contends that, unless there really are common natures which are less-than-numerically one, then the similarities and differences we observe in nature will simply be mind-dependent. If there is no real common nature of horseness shared by Black Beauty and Bucephalus (and, because shared, less-than-numerically one), then Black Beauty and Bucephalus are alike just because that is how they appear to us.

Scotus produces some powerful arguments to support his view. For instance, he asks us to consider what is really the opposite of a black thing. It must be white, and it must be a real thing too (if it is really opposite), and, since everything real is one—a maxim everyone accepted—it must be one. But it is not numerically one, since it is not as if there were only one white thing really opposite to this black thing: *any* white thing is its opposite. It is true that Scotus' justification for less-than-numerical unity supposes that no other form of realism is tenable, but Scotus does give detailed arguments against the other existing theories.

Scotus has also to explain what makes Black Beauty and Bucephalus, who share the common nature horseness, into individual horses. He argues against seeing accidents, matter, or something merely negative as the principle of individuation, and is left with the view that each individual is indeed individuated by an individuator (sometimes called, especially after Scotus' time, a 'haecceity'—that is, a thisness), which 'contracts' the common nature into an individual. But the two entities within the individual, the common nature and the individuator, are not, he says, distinguished as thing and thing, but merely, as he describes it, 'formally'. There is just one thing, Black Beauty, for example, which has two formally distinct realities: the common nature of horseness, and an individuator.

Ockham: nominalism again

William of Ockham rejected Scotus' baroque apparatus of individuators and formal distinctions. Two items, he insisted, can be distinguished only as thing and thing, concept and concept, or thing and concept. Scotus' theory depends on being able to hold both that Black Beauty's nature is different from what individuates him, and that this nature and the individuator are not different things from one another, nor therefore from Black Beauty himself.

By rejecting the distinctions on which Scotus' position rests, Ockham can find many arguments against it. For example, from Ockham's perspective, Scotus must hold that Black Beauty is not different from his nature, horseness, because they are not different things. But Black Beauty is a different thing from Bucephalus (which is also not different from its nature). Black Beauty's nature is therefore a different thing from Bucephalus' nature. So every horse will have to have its own nature (and, says Ockham, its own species)—an absurd conclusion.

Ockham rejected not just Scotus' but every variety of realism. Universals, he argued (like Abelard, whose works he did not

know), are not things in the world. Rather, they are unreal mental objects or, as he came to think later, they are identical to our acts of thinking them. Ockham sees no need to introduce anything like Abelard's *status*: it is enough for these mental universals to refer to all the particulars which fall under them. He conceives them as terms in a mental language, which are naturally linked to the things for which they stand. Whereas the word 'horse' in English applies to horses merely by convention, the mentalese term HORSE is somehow fitted (by similarity and through causality, he suggests) to stand for all and only horses.

Ockham's nominalism (and the somewhat different, nominalist theory developed a little later by John Buridan in Paris) did not settle the problem. Universals were the subject of lively controversy in the late 14th and 15th centuries, and perhaps the most sophisticated and complex solution to the problems they raise was given at the very end of the 16th century by Suárez. Suárez drew especially on Ockham and Scotus, but he was joining in an intellectual conversation the terms of which went back much further, certainly as far as Alexander of Aphrodisias and, through him, to Aristotle.

Chapter 7
Mind, body, and mortality (Averroes and Pomponazzi)

In Chapter 6 it was possible, after explaining a little terminology, to move straight from a general description of the problem of universals, which a philosopher today would recognize, to Avicenna and Abelard. In this chapter, about theories of mind and body, the medieval discussions are less close to today's debate. The reason for this distance may be surprising. It is not, as many would think, because of religious ideas about the immortality of the soul. In fact, both Jewish and Muslim orthodox doctrine about immortality concerns the resurrection of the whole person (many *kalām* theologians were indeed thoroughgoing materialists). And, although the Catholic Church did insist that human souls survive separately from the body, there were Christian thinkers ready to reject this position within philosophy, even though they accepted it as a revealed dogma. The distance from the contemporary problem is, rather, the result of the Aristotelian framework within which most medieval thinkers thought about mind and body, and the cosmological view of intellectual understanding developed by his interpreters.

Aristotle on the soul, intellectual knowledge, and immortality

The contemporary problem of mind and body does not square up with the Aristotelian and medieval discussion of the same

area. For us, Descartes's division (which has a good deal in common with Plato's) seems the obvious one, even when we reject entirely the dualism he derives from it. On the one side, there is the mind, by which we mean consciousness—thoughts, mental images, sensations, pains—on the other side, the body, a highly complex machine. Aristotle did not make this division. Rather, he began by thinking about the make-up of any substance, living or not.

In his *Categories* (as discussed in Chapter 6) Aristotle distinguishes between substances and accidents. But, in other writings, he also analyses how substances themselves are composed: they are, he says, combinations of substantial form and matter. Matter is mere potentiality, which does not actually exist without a form. Substantial form is what the thing is: the stoneness, for instance, which makes this thing into a stone. Substantial forms correspond to species, but—although the question is much debated—Aristotle did not seem to regard them as universals (Avicenna's doctrine of natures thus clarifies Aristotle's theory).

In the case of a stone, the form might be said to be that which accounts for how the matter is configured in order for it to be a stone. But a tree is more complicated. What it is to be a tree is not just to be configured in a certain way, but also to have certain life activities—growing from a seed, sprouting leaves, reproducing. The form of a tree accounts for its life activities and is called by Aristotle its 'soul'. Similarly, the form of a horse is its soul, and it accounts not just for its physical structure and its growing, but its ability to move, to perceive with the senses, and to seek some things, such as food, and avoid others, such as fire. Human beings too each have a soul as their substantial form: it accounts not only for the life activities they share with plants and other animals—growing, sensing, and the internal sense-activity of imagining and remembering—but also for their unique ability, among bodily things, to engage in intellectual reasoning.

For Aristotle, then, there is a fundamental distinction between non-living and living things. Though both share the same matter and form structure, only living things have souls. He makes no sharp distinction between beings without and with consciousness. In humans, much of their conscious activity belongs to the aspect of their soul which they share with other animals—pains, sense perceptions, even imaginary visual images and their combination. All this activity is considered to depend on the functioning of physical organs: the sense organs such as ears and eyes, and the internal senses which are situated in the brain.

There is, however, one activity of humans which Aristotle *does* sharply distinguish from anything done by non-human animals: the reasoning which is the activity of the intellect. The intellect, according to Aristotle, reasons about universals and their interrelations in a logical way so as to form a scientific theory. Just as the senses perceive by being informed by particular, sensible forms (this smell, that visual image), so the intellect receives universal forms (such as the stoneness which, particularized, makes a stone what it is) and reasons with them. It is entirely in potency, until it receives a form. But these forms, by contrast with the forms received by the sense organs, are immaterial, although Aristotle adds that humans cannot use their intellects without also having accompanying sensory images.

Aristotle's conception of the intellect complicates his view of the relation between souls and bodies. It would seem that, through his very conception of souls as the forms of living things, Aristotle has ruled out dualism, and any possibility of the soul's survival after the death of the body. How can a form exist when that of which it is a form has perished? Aristotle himself judges it 'not unclear' that 'neither the soul nor certain parts of it, if it has parts, can be separated from the body'. Yet it turns out that matters are not so simple.

Aristotle does explicitly leave open at least the theoretical possibility that parts of the soul *could* be separated from the body

if they were not themselves 'actualities' of the body—that is to say, if they did not act as its form and had a function separate from that of the body. He also says that as well as the intellect which receives forms (the 'possible' or 'material' intellect, which is entirely in potency), there is an active intellect, which makes all things, and which is 'separable and impassive and unmixed'. But it is unclear whether Aristotle is still talking about human cognition here at all and, if so, whether the active intellect is a part of each human's soul or a single, external thing.

The Arabic Aristotelian tradition

Although the late ancient Greek commentators reached no consensus on the matter, the Arabic Aristotelians were agreed that the active intellect is a single, separate, eternal, and incorporeal being. In the tradition up to Averroes, the active intellect was given a place within a scheme devised by al-Fārābī, which brought together Aristotle's metaphysics and psychology, the Neoplatonism of Proclus, and the Ptolemaic conception of the universe as consisting of nine concentric spheres. From God, the First Cause, there emanates a First Intelligence, which is responsible for producing both the first, outermost sphere, which it moves, and the following Intelligence. This process is repeated until, from the Intelligence of the ninth sphere there emanates the final, lowest Intelligence, which is the Active (or, as it is often called, 'Agent') Intellect. It neither produces another Intelligence nor a sphere: its role is in our world (the 'sublunar world', because it is below the lowest sphere, that of the moon), both—according to some of these thinkers—in bestowing forms to matter and so ensuring the eternal process of generation and decay, and in enabling human intellects to grasp universals (see Figure 8).

All the universals, and so a complete, scientific understanding of reality, were held to be contained in complete unity in the First Cause and transmitted down the chain of celestial intelligences to the Agent Intellect. In Avicenna, this scheme leads to an account

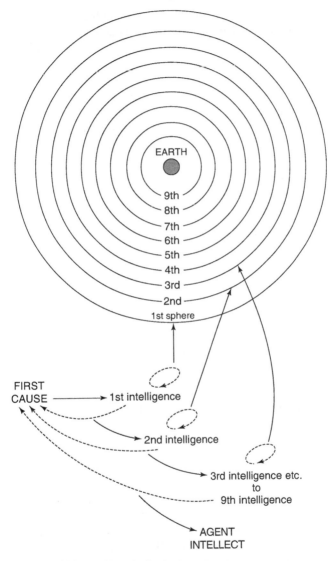

EARTH

9th
8th
7th
6th
5th
4th
3rd
2nd
1st sphere

FIRST
CAUSE → 1st intelligence

2nd intelligence

3rd intelligence etc.
to
9th intelligence

AGENT
INTELLECT

Mind, body, and mortality

8. Al-Fārābī's cosmological scheme.

of intellectual cognition which fits uneasily with his theory of universals. We begin from our sense perceptions and, by collecting and abstracting, arrive at a purified image of, for instance, Horse. When the preparatory work of abstraction is done in the imagination (and so in a corporeal organ, the brain), the Agent Intellect joins to our (incorporeal) possible intellect so that we can grasp the nature in question within it, as transmitted down, ultimately from the universal idea of it in the mind of God. Avicenna even denies that, having grasped them, we can store these concepts; rather, through habituation we find it easier to make the required link with the Agent Intellect.

With regard to the possible intellect, there was general agreement among Greek commentators and among the philosophers in Islam before (and after) Averroes, that each human has his own. Since cognition, in the Aristotelian tradition, requires the assimilation of what is cognized, it was thought that nothing bodily could be what receives and knows universals. The possible intellect was therefore considered to be incorporeal (but could be called 'material' in the sense that it receives forms). Avicenna uses the incorporeality of the possible intellect as an argument for its immortality, but there was a minority view, put by Alexander of Aphrodisias, that it perishes along with the body it informs.

Averroes on the intellect, mortality, and immortality

Averroes broke with the whole interpretative tradition when, after taking (in his earlier works) a position similar to that of Alexander of Aphrodisias, he developed the view in his Great Commentary concerning *On the Soul* that not only is there just one active intellect, but also there is only one possible (or 'material') intellect for all humans. Both of these intellects are separate, immaterial things, of a sort unlike anything in the sublunar world: neither form nor matter, nor a composite of form and matter. On the face of it, Averroes seems to be saying that all humans share a single

mind—an obviously absurd view. But his real position is much more interesting and plausible.

Averroes' starting point is that the possible intellect which receives universal forms must be immaterial. Were it bodily, the intellect would receive forms in the way bodies do, making them into individuals, whereas its function is to grasp these forms as universals. So far, Averroes has merely stated what almost every Aristotelian accepted. But he then brings in another Aristotelian principle: that which individuates things is bodily matter. But the possible intellect is not bodily, and so it cannot be individuated, with one intellect for each human: there must be just a single intellect for all humans.

This unity brings some explanatory benefits. It shows why, when you and I learn mathematics or astronomy, it is one and the same science. But there seems also to be an unacceptably high explanatory cost. If I learn astronomy, it does not follow that you have also learned it: our learning and knowing are individual to each of us and depend on our efforts. Averroes has to explain how individual humans are related to the single intellect in such a way as to respect the individuality of our knowledge.

Like Avicenna, Averroes thinks that is the senses, external and internal, which do the work that enable us to grasp universals, preparing stripped-down, imaginative forms, which are almost like universals but still remain imaginative, and therefore corporeal, forms. At this point, for Avicenna, a person will receive in his or her own possible intellect the universal form from the Agent Intellect. For Averroes, what happens is almost the reverse. He explains it by using an analogy from sensation. Suppose I have a sense perception of the white of this cup in front of me. The sense perception requires two things in order for it to exist as a sense perception of this cup's whiteness: the white cup itself, and my sense of sight. They are both the subjects of the sensation (in the same way that the cup is the subject of the accident of

whiteness that inheres in it). Similarly, for the act of grasping the universal Horse, there are two subjects: the stripped-down, imaginative forms of horses supplied by my sensory imaginative powers, and the possible intellect (which is one and exists apart from me and all other humans). My imaginative forms play the role of the white cup in the analogy: without them the understanding would not be, as Averroes says, 'true'. The possible intellect plays the role of my sense of sight in the analogy: just as a visual perception cannot exist except in a sense organ, so an immaterial universal cannot exist except in an immaterial (and so, for Averroes, not an individuated) thing which cognizes it.

Averroes explains the role of the active intellect in this process by another analogy. For me to see a coloured object, the air between it and my eyes need to be filled with the colour, and this happens only when there is light shining on the object. In a similar way, the Agent Intellect, like the sun, illuminates the stripped-down imaginative forms in my inner senses, making them into the universals which fill the possible intellect.

An intellectual cognition of a universal (for instance, of Horse) is mine, therefore, if I am supplying the stripped-down sense images on which it is based, and this is something which Averroes believes is at our will and to some extent within each of our powers, and is an ability we can improve as we study the world and apply ourselves to learning. He does not picture the active intellect as merely acting on us from afar, using the images we each supply but having no further connection with us. Rather, in an act of intellectual cognition, the active intellect is conjoined with the person who supplies the images. The more fully someone engages in the pursuit of knowledge and masters the sciences, the closer and more complete the conjunction, which, Averroes believes, provides complete human fulfilment and happiness.

The boldest stroke in the theory, however, becomes evident only in the light of Averroes' wider metaphysical position in his later

years. He abandoned the Platonically influenced theory of emanation developed by al-Fārābī and used by Avicenna. He accepts, following Aristotle, that there is a First Mover, and that there are intelligences which move the celestial spheres. But they do so because of their desire for the most perfect being, the First Mover, just as Aristotle himself had said. The role of the active intellect as the giver of forms to the sublunar world is dropped.

Moreover, since the First Mover contemplates only itself, and knows other things only in so far as it is their cause, universal concepts cannot be passed down from it to the active intellect. Rather, the active intellect is presented purely as a power for rendering the stripped-down images prepared by humans universal in the possible intellect, which is in itself an empty, pure receiver. Humans do not have their own intellects, on Averroes' view, but, equally, without humans there is no intellectual cognition. The images humans provide are not merely an element in the cognitive process: they are its content.

There is, therefore, a slight disanalogy with the case of perception: I could have a visual perception—a misleading one—of white even if there were no white thing in front of me. But the possible intellect cannot be informed with the universal Horse unless there is some human to supply stripped-down images of horse. It is for this reason that Averroes takes pains to explain that at every time there will be a philosopher somewhere in the world; if there were not, the proper function of the active and material intellects would cease. In a way that the usual descriptions of his theory would never suggest, Averroes puts human beings more firmly at the centre of his view of the universe than any thinker—since Aristotle.

Thomas Aquinas and the reaction to Averroes' theory

Averroes' Great Commentary concerning *On the Soul* survived and was diffused only in the Latin tradition (until the late Middle

Ages, when it was translated from the Latin into Hebrew). By following an Avicennian reading of the text, and identifying the active intellect with God himself, Latin theologians of the early 13th century had been able to absorb what they took to be Aristotle's views without much difficulty. Once, by the mid-century, they read and properly understood Averroes' theory, they denounced it, since it clearly denied individual immortality to disembodied human souls. By contrast, a number of Arts Masters were convinced that it was the best interpretation of *On the Soul* and, following their role as expositors of Aristotle, adopted it, though they accepted that the truth, according to Christian doctrine, was otherwise.

The most powerful attack on Averroes' theory came from Thomas Aquinas. He pointed out that Averroes' view went against the entire tradition of interpreting Aristotle's *On the Soul*. He also argued that it was philosophically unacceptable. On Averroes' theory, Aquinas contends, the relationship between the active intellect and the individual human, whose stripped-down images the active intellect transforms into universals in the possible intellect, is like that of an eye to a wall, the colour of which it is seeing. But we say that the eye sees the coloured wall, not that the wall is seeing. And so, Aquinas concludes, in Averroes' scheme it is the separate intellect which cognizes the human, rather than the human having intellectual cognition. Averroes, though, could reply that the analogy is not exact: unlike the human, the wall is not a voluntary contributor to the act of cognition.

Aquinas himself resembled Averroes in his wish strictly to follow Aristotle's view that the human soul and body are related as matter and form, but he insisted that the intellect (both active and potential) is fully a part of the human soul; indeed, although it has other powers, the human soul is an *intellective* soul. By linking the intellective soul so closely to the human body as its unique substantial form, Aquinas gave an attractively unified view of the

human person. It was not, however, easy for him to show how, given that it is the body's form, the soul can survive without it. His argument is that it can, because its characteristic activity is intellectual reasoning, for which, unlike perceiving or imagining, no bodily organ is required.

By contrast, most of the Christian theologians of Aquinas' time held that humans have at least two substantial forms: the soul, and a substantial form for the body. This un-Aristotelian dualism made it easy for them to explain the soul's survival and immortality. This approach, in various sophisticated versions, was the most popular among later medieval theologians. Arts Masters, however, often opted for Averroes' view or an adaptation of it, although it had been attacked by theologians and officially condemned. Their Averroism was usually tolerated, so long as they made sure to add that, despite Aristotle's views, Christian doctrine on the soul's immortality is true. Some, like John Buridan, preferred Alexander of Aphrodisias' view, that the human soul, like that of other animals, is mortal, as the best interpretation of the text and the most convincing doctrine rationally—though to be rejected as false, because it contradicts Christian teaching.

Pomponazzi on the mortality of the soul

In his treatise *On the Immortality of the Soul*, published in 1516, Pomponazzi quickly dismisses Averroes' views, and also those of Ficino, who had turned to Plato to provide arguments for the soul's immortality. But he examines Aquinas' position in detail. He queries, as Averroists or any good Aristotelians would, how it is possible for disembodied human souls to be individuated, since individuation is by matter. His main criticism, though, is directed against Aquinas' claim that the human intellective soul can be the form of the body and yet also sufficiently detached from it to survive on its own.

Pomponazzi observes that, while one of its activities, intellectual thought, does not require a bodily organ, and so suggests it could be separated from the body, its other activities, such as sensing, do require bodily organs and so provide equally strong reason to think that it cannot survive separately. If human intellectual activity is really, as Aquinas contends, independent of the body, then the human soul will not be, as it must be if it is the human's substantial form, that which explains a bodily human being's life activities ('the act of an organic body'). Pomponazzi also points to the weakness of Aquinas' claim that the embodied human soul uses sense images in the process of intellectual cognition, whereas in its separate state the same soul can cognize without them. Would it really be the same soul, and, if it has the power to dispense with images, why can it not do so when it is embodied?

According to Pomponazzi, Aquinas holds that the human soul is unqualifiedly immortal and mortal in a qualified sense (in that its vegetative and sensitive aspects are mortal). The position he himself proposes and defends is, rather, that the human soul is unqualifiedly mortal and immortal in a qualified sense. This qualified immortality is merely humans' ability to grasp eternal, unchanging things. There are, says Pomponazzi, three degrees to which different types of cognition can be separated from matter. The intelligences are completely separate from matter in their way of knowing. By contrast, there are the powers of sensory perception. Although sensory perception does not, in his view, involve material reception—since sight, for instance, takes on not the objects themselves it sees, but likenesses of them—it is completely rooted in the material world, which provides both its object, the things sensed, and its subject: the corporeal sense organs.

Between the two is the human intellect. It is not based in a sense organ as its subject, but it requires a sense organ—the imagination—as its object, since Aristotle insists that we cannot engage in intellectual cognition without an accompaniment of

images in the imagination. It is perhaps the weight Pomponazzi places on this requirement which, more than anything, explains how his views diverge from Aquinas'. Both thinkers agree that human intellection is an immaterial power, not that of a bodily organ. But, urges Pomponazzi, since it cannot function without the working of the imagination (situated in the brain), it cannot survive the body.

Pomponazzi defends his position energetically. As well as answering direct counterarguments to his interpretation of Aristotle, he responds to wider objections against the mortalist consequences of his position. If there is no life after death, and so no reward or punishment, then why should people ever choose to die for their country, or indeed not be willing to commit any crime, however horrible, to save their lives? Pomponazzi answers that the true reward for virtue is virtue itself. Those who act well in the hope of some extrinsic reward, such as blessedness in heaven, are less than fully virtuous. To the objection that all the religions of the world uphold the immortality of the soul, and so Pomponazzi is in the weak position of holding that almost everyone else is wrong, he answers with a straight face that, supposing there are just three religions—Christianity, Judaism, and Islam—then either they are false, and so everyone is mistaken, or at least two of them are, and so most people are mistaken.

It is on account of comments such as this that Pomponazzi is seen by some as a precursor of the Enlightenment, whose aim was to undermine religious belief. Just like the many Arts Masters who followed Averroes' views about the intellect, Pomponazzi overtly distances himself from the position he defends with vigour and accepts that Christian teaching about immortality (and indeed Aquinas' interpretation of it!) is, in fact, the truth.

But, these interpreters say, here Pomponazzi is simply doing what was necessary, if he was to publish his work and not be condemned as a heretic. Yet there are good grounds for taking his

framing statements at face value. Pomponazzi contends that he has shown that the immortality of the soul is not defended by Aristotle, and that it is not something which can be demonstrated; nor can the mortality of the soul (and none of the arguments he gives for it were claimed to be demonstrations). It is therefore a neutral problem, as Aquinas himself had described the question of the eternity of the world. Reason cannot give a definite verdict one way or the other, and so it is reasonable to turn to faith, which can answer with certainty.

Pomponazzi's courage lies not in an attempt to undermine religion but in his opposition to the increasing tendency of the Church, in his time, to demand that thinkers find rational arguments to support specifically Christian teaching and to counter heterodox views. And this was a demand Pomponazzi constantly refused, insisting against the Church authorities on both the limitations of human reason, and its autonomy within its own sphere.

Chapter 8
Foreknowledge and freedom (Boethius and Gersonides)

The problem of future truth

Most people take it for granted that some future events are contingent—that is to say, they might or might not take place. In particular, we usually consider that matters over which we exercise choice are contingent: for example, whether or not I drink wine tomorrow. If this event is not contingent, and my drinking wine tomorrow or my not drinking wine tomorrow is fixed, and not something which might or might not take place, then how can it be a matter of my choice? Yet, as was first pointed out by Aristotle in *On Interpretation*, there is a problem. If the sentence 'Tomorrow John Marenbon will drink wine' is true now, then it is now the case that I shall drink wine tomorrow. It is not open for me not to do so; or if it is false, then it is not open for me to do so. But sentences, we normally consider, must be either true or false—one or the other: there is no middle way. And so neither my drinking wine tomorrow nor, by the same argument, any future event is contingent.

There are various ways of tackling this difficulty: the most straightforward is simply to drop the assumption that sentences about future contingents must be either true or false. This chapter is concerned with the more difficult problem, the 'problem of (divine) prescience', which arises when an omniscient God (a God who knows everything), such as that of the Platonists, Jews,

Christians, and Muslims, is added to the picture. If God knows all things, he knows whether or not I shall drink wine tomorrow, and, because he is unchanging, he has known so from all eternity. Consequently, this event cannot turn out other than God foreknows it. It is not, as it seems, contingent, and so I have no choice whether or not to drink wine tomorrow. There is no obvious escape route, as in the case of the truth of sentences, because—at least according to most thinkers—a perfect, infinitely wise God cannot lack such knowledge. After more than 2,000 years of discussion, this problem of prescience still exercises philosophers of religion.

Contingency, necessity, and free will

Two preliminary explanations are needed for understanding the problem of prescience as it was discussed in the Middle Ages: about the Aristotelian way of conceiving contingency and necessity, and about compatibilism and incompatibilism.

Necessity and contingency. Ancient, medieval, and contemporary philosophers are united in accepting that, if something is contingent, then it is neither necessary nor impossible (what is impossible is necessarily not the case). But philosophers today have a different understanding of necessity itself. They are most interested in what they call 'logical' necessity, in connection with sentences. A sentence is logically necessary if and only if its negation is a contradiction (for example: '2 + 2 = 4'; 'If he is a bachelor, he is unmarried'). They will also sometimes talk about physical necessity and physical impossibility: for example, it is physically impossible for me to fly by my own power. Neither of these senses quite captures the broad meaning of 'necessary' in the Aristotelian tradition.

In the Aristotelian tradition, events are necessary which cannot be otherwise, in the sense that nothing can be done to alter them. A favourite example of a necessary event in the Aristotelian tradition is that the sun will rise tomorrow—this is, in contemporary terms,

physically necessary. But it is also necessary in Aristotelian terms that I drank wine yesterday because nothing can change that now, whereas philosophers now would not consider it necessary (except, some would allow, 'accidentally'). Medieval philosophers usually discuss the problem of prescience using an Aristotelian understanding of necessity, although Duns Scotus, as will be explained, is led by the problem to reject Aristotle's view.

Compatibilism and incompatibilism. The conclusion that all future events are necessary is disturbing mainly because it seems to leave no room for human free will. If it is necessary that I drink wine tomorrow, it seems that I cannot choose to be abstinent. Some philosophers, however, do not accept this consequence. These 'compatibilists' say that we are free so long we exercise our wills and make choices, even if these choices could not in fact have been other than they are. Aristotle clearly assumed the opposite 'incompatibilist' position: that, if the future is necessary and so we do not have real alternative choices, then we have no freedom and are not therefore responsible for actions and cannot justly be rewarded or punished for them.

The extent to which some medieval philosophers accepted compatibilism is debated by historians, but in tackling the problem of prescience, most were unwilling to follow the radical strategy of accepting that everything happens of necessity and going on to vindicate human freedom by appeal to compatibilism. Rather, they usually tried to find some way of reconciling divine omniscience with contingent future events.

Boethius' solution to the problem of prescience

In the last book of his *Consolation of Philosophy*, Boethius, who had earlier discussed the logical problem of the truth of sentences about future contingents when commenting on Aristotle's *On Interpretation*, tackles the problem of prescience. He is not disturbed by what seems to be the obvious

formulation of the problem: that, if God knows now what I shall do tomorrow—for example, that I shall drink wine—then, since anything that is *known* cannot be false, I shall necessarily drink wine tomorrow.

Boethius makes clear that he is leaving aside God's role in bringing about events (God as predestiner) and looking just at his foreknowledge. Then he explains that what makes beliefs, including knowledge, true is that they correspond with how things are: their being true cannot make things be in a certain way. If an event is contingent, then God's foreknowing it cannot make it necessary.

There is, however, a different way of posing the problem which, Boethius thinks, is much less easy to answer. For someone to know something it is not enough to have a belief that happens to be true; the knower needs to be in a position to be sure that the belief is indeed true. This certainty requires that what is known is fixed and determinate. Assume that there are contingent future events. Such events are precisely those which do not have a fixed outcome, and so, although they might be the object of true belief, there cannot be knowledge about them. Either, then, (a) we must say that God can merely believe about a future contingent event that it will happen in such a way that it might not have happened. Even if this belief happens to be true, it will not be knowledge. Or (b) we shall have to say that, when God truly believes about a contingent event that it will happen, he believes falsely that it will happen in such a way that it could not fail to happen. Since neither alternative can be true of an all-knowing God, the assumption that gave rise to them must be rejected: no future events are contingent.

Boethius' solution to this version of the problem is based on a surprising move. He accepts the second of the alternatives, (b), that God believes about true contingent events that they happen and cannot fail to happen, that is, they will happen necessarily. Yet

he rejects the contention that such divine beliefs are false. But how can it not be false to judge contingent events to be necessary? Boethius' answer is that, in judging the truth of a cognizer's belief, we must consider the sort of cognizer it is and how it cognizes. Analysis of the relationship between time, events, and God's way of cognition, shows that, when God cognizes an event which is, in itself, contingent, the event is necessary from God's point of view.

On the Aristotelian view, contingency and necessity are affected by an event's temporal position in relation to us. Many future events, such as my drinking wine tomorrow, are contingent, because they may turn out one way or the other. As soon as an event happens, however, it is necessary because it cannot be otherwise. But God's relation to time, Boethius explains, is unlike ours. To say that God is eternal does not mean simply that his existence has neither beginning nor end. God's eternity, he says (in a phrase which became standard in medieval theology) 'is the complete, simultaneous and perfect possession of unending life'.

Some interpreters today take this to mean that, according to Boethius, God is atemporal—outside time altogether. But this reading is improbable, since Boethius clearly conceives God's life as having duration. What Boethius does make clear, however, is that, because he is eternal, God knows in a special way, which reflects the way in which his relationship to events in time is different from ours. He knows all events—whether they are, for us, past, present, or future—in the way that we know present events. When, therefore, God foreknows that I shall drink a glass of wine tomorrow, he knows it in the same way that you might know it at the time, if you are there at table with me in front of your eyes. It is not really, Boethius explains, *fore*knowledge at all, but knowledge of what, from God's point of view, is the present. This is why the event, although contingent in itself, is necessary as cognized by God: what is happening at the present moment, and so also what is known to be happening at the present moment, is necessary, because it cannot be otherwise.

But does not this necessity of the event, as known by God, remove human freedom to change it? No, Boethius replies: the necessity of the present, or of knowledge of the present, does not limit freedom. The fact that you are watching me drink this glass of wine and know I am doing so does not make my drinking any less free. This is because my freedom lies in my being able to bring it about that, at the next moment, I stop drinking, not in my being able to change what is now the case. Similarly, the fact that God knows all my intentions and deeds, past, present, and future, in what is to him the present, does not make me any less free.

After Boethius

Abelard thought that there was a much simpler solution to the problem of prescience than Boethius'. He thought that the problem to be faced was what we called earlier the 'obvious' one: that, if God knows now that I shall, for instance, drink wine tomorrow, then, since anything that is *known* cannot be false, I shall necessarily drink wine tomorrow. He rightly pointed out that this argument rests on a logical error. What follows from the fact that knowledge must, by definition, be of the truth is just that the whole 'if…then' statement 'If God knows now I shall drink wine tomorrow, then I shall drink wine tomorrow' is necessarily true. So, if the antecedent ('God knows now I shall drink wine tomorrow') is true, then it follows necessarily that the consequent ('I shall drink wine tomorrow') is true, but not that it is necessarily true.

Abelard, however, was too impressed by his own ability to notice a fallacy. His solution does not solve the problem of prescience, because he has not taken proper account (as Boethius, in his own way, had done) of its temporal element. Before the mid-13th century theologians had begun to formulate the problem in a tight, logical way, which recognized its temporal element and was not touched by Abelard's pseudo-solution. All they had to do was

to show that the antecedent ('God knows now I shall drink wine tomorrow') is itself not merely true, but necessarily true, since it was accepted (as it is, usually, by logicians now) that what follows of necessity from a proposition that is itself necessary will also be necessarily true. So, if it is, not just contingently the case, but necessary that God knows I shall drink wine tomorrow, then it follows that my drinking wine tomorrow is necessary, and so my freedom to abstain is delusory. And there were two good reasons for the theologians to consider that the antecedent is indeed necessary. First, God is immutable, and so whatever he knows, he knows always and unchangingly, and this amounted, according to their understanding, to his knowledge being necessary. Second, since God is immutable, that I shall drink wine tomorrow is something he already knows: it is a fact about the past. And facts about the past are, in Aristotelian terms, necessary.

In this form, the problem of prescience was very challenging. Aquinas recognized the difficulty very clearly, but his solution, following the lines of Boethius', does not fully meet it. Duns Scotus chose, rather, to tackle the problem from a completely different angle. Boethius and Aquinas had both kept the problem of prescience completely separate from the related, and even more difficult, problem of God's providence. Christians (and Jews, Muslims, and Platonists) believe that God does not merely know how humans will act, he providentially arranges the world for them. In the form in which most medieval Christians understood the doctrine, God does not merely know that I shall drink wine tomorrow: it is part of the providence he has willed that I shall do so. None the less, drinking the wine will be my own free choice. Scotus attached his answer to the problem of prescience to his solution concerning this even more difficult problem.

Unless God himself wills not necessarily but contingently, Scotus argued, there can be no contingency at all in the universe, since God is the ultimate source of everything that happens. But, on the

Aristotelian conception of necessity, it turns out to be impossible for God to will contingently. On this conception, a will must be able to change at least once from one instant to another in order not to be necessary. Suppose this instant is the only one of my existence, then whatever I am willing now I am willing necessarily, since nothing can change what I am willing now in this instant (the Aristotelian necessity of the present) and my existence does not stretch beyond it. But God, according to the conception Scotus and his contemporaries shared, is in just this position. Many of them (unlike Aquinas) believed that he exists in a timeless instant; in any case, all accepted that he is immutable, and so, even if his existence covers infinitely many instants, his will cannot change from one to another.

Scotus decided therefore to abandon the Aristotelian conception of necessity, in favour of a view nearer to the idea of logical possibility and necessity held by many philosophers now. The present is no longer considered to be necessary, because, although nothing can change the fact that I am now willing to drink wine, it might have been—according to another, synchronically possible state of affairs—that I was not willing to drink it at this moment. Scotus contends that, as well as my obvious power to will otherwise than I do by changing my will (as in the Aristotelian picture), I have the much less obvious power to be willing at this very moment the opposite of what I am in fact willing. God, who is immutable and exists in an instant, has this second power (though not the first), and so his will is contingent.

Indeed, Scotus distinguishes two 'instants of nature', or non-temporal, logical stages. In the first, God knows all the different ways in which the universe could possibly be. In the second, he chooses one complete history of the universe out of the infinite possible histories and wills that it should be the actual one. He foreknows the future by knowing which history his will has chosen. Still, even accepting Scotus' modal innovations and his instants of nature—as Ockham, for example, would not—in this complete world history

freely chosen by God there will be freedom for humans only on compatibilist assumptions.

Before Gersonides

Christian theologians were doctrinally committed to holding that God's knowledge extends to particular things and events, and hence, because it is complete, to future contingents. By contrast, in the Arabic philosophical tradition and among Jewish philosophers, there was room to deny God direct knowledge of particulars and so of contingent events past and present, as well as future. Avicenna held that God knows particulars only in a universal way: he knows, by knowing himself, universals and the principles of all things, of which he is cause. Averroes also believes that God's knowledge of other things is a knowledge of himself as their cause, but he denies that God knows in either a particular or a universal way. Divine knowledge is, he says, totally unlike ours.

Maimonides considers that it is essential to Jewish teaching that God without qualification knows every particular and event, including future contingent ones. He is fully aware of the problem about how such foreknown events can still be contingent. But he tackles this difficulty in a way quite different from the logical arguments of the Latin tradition. It is, rather, similar to Averroes', although the position he uses it to justify is not at all the same.

Maimonides turns to one of his own central ideas. Neoplatonic, Christian, Jewish, and Arabic thinkers had developed a negative theology: the view that human language is inadequate for talking about God, and so it is more accurate to describe God by saying what he is not than what he is. Maimonides proposes a very strict version of this negative theology (which was influential on Christian thinkers, such as Aquinas, but moderated by them). According to him, we use human language equivocally (as 'bank' is

used equivocally in 'high-street bank' and 'bank of the Thames') when we talk about God. When, therefore, we say that 'God knows future contingent events', we should not be misled by the verbal similarity between 'knows' in this statement and the same word in sentences such as 'John knows it is raining' or 'John knows $2 + 2 = 4$', because 'knows' is being used equivocally. According to Maimonides, we simply do not comprehend what it means for God to know something, although we can gain some glimmer of understanding by thinking of the special grasp a maker has of what he makes. His answer to the problem of prescience is, then, that God knows future contingent events and we do not, and *cannot*, know how.

Gersonides on Maimonides

Gersonides was aware of the views of Averroes, and he thought that a view close to Avicenna's was the correct interpretation of Aristotle. But he was much more concerned with Maimonides: indeed, he wrote his philosophical masterpiece, the *Wars of the Lord*, to address topics which, he thought, had been inadequately treated in Maimonides' *Guide of the Perplexed*. Gersonides dismisses his answer to the problem of prescience by rejecting the negative theology on which it is based.

If words used about God are really equivocal in the strict sense Maimonides claims, then any affirmation or denial about God is equally appropriate. So, for instance, 'God is a body' would be perfectly acceptable, since the meaning of 'body', of which we are ignorant, has nothing to do with its ordinary meaning. Moreover, Gersonides points out that, on Maimonides' theory of pure equivocation, the central strategy of negative theology becomes impossible. Negative theology takes predicates we use of things other than God and says they are not true of God. But if such words have a completely different meaning when applied to God than when used otherwise, what grounds can there be for saying that they are not true of him?

Gersonides' own solution to the problem of prescience

Although Gersonides rejects Maimonides' way of escaping the problem of prescience, he agrees with him (by contrast with most thinkers in the Latin tradition) that there can be no philosophical explanation of how an event can be foreknown and yet contingent. He solves the problem by looking at it within the wider context of God's knowledge of particulars. With the problem not just of God's foreknowledge but his immutability in mind—how can God know changing things without himself changing?— Gersonides concludes that God 'knows particulars in one respect but does not know them in another respect'. He does not know them as particulars, but he does know them 'in so far as they are ordered and determined'.

The meaning of this distinction is explained by Gersonides' theory of providence. Unlike Averroes in his mature work, Gersonides accepts the full Avicennian theory of emanation from God, the first cause, through to the Agent Intellect, which transmits forms to the sublunar world. In this way, the broad patterns of how things happen in the world are part of God's order. But, with regard to humans (and humans alone: for Gersonides there is *no* providence in the fall of a sparrow), he believes that God's providential ordering extends far further. Gersonides, who was famous as an astronomer, accepted astral determinism. Through the positioning of the stars, God providentially controls human affairs, not just in their broad outlines but in their details: they too, then, are ordered and determined. God, then, is able to know particular events concerning humans and their actions, but he knows them, not as particular events, but as part of his providential order.

From what has been said so far, it will seem that Gersonides may be able to explain divine prescience, but only at the cost of

sacrificing human freedom, since our actions are determined by the stars. But in fact he makes an important exception to astral determinism. By using their intellects, humans are able to act contrary to the way the stars determine. Suppose that, as astrally determined, I am addicted to alcohol, and my wine drinking is damaging my ability to lead a worthwhile life. The stars, then, have determined that I shall drink wine tomorrow, but, according to Gersonides, it still lies in my power for me to reason that it would be better if tomorrow is alcohol free for me and then *not* to drink wine tomorrow. God knows that I, like other humans, have this power, but he does not know whether I shall exercise it.

God's knowledge of his creation is therefore limited in three ways. First, with regard to non-human behaviour he knows only the broad laws which govern it. Second, although he knows in detail human behaviour controlled through the stars, through knowing its detailed causal principles, his knowledge includes the proviso that any event may not come about in the way determined by these principles, because humans have the power of free choice. Third, God therefore does not know with regard to human acts which of the two contradictory outcomes will in fact be the case: whether or not, for instance, the alcoholic will overcome his yearning for wine so that he does not drink it tomorrow. And it seems also that God, whose knowledge is unchanging, never even comes to know about such particular, contingent actions.

To the suggestion that God is thus less than perfect, it can be answered that, for Gersonides, in the strict sense things are known only when the reasons for them are grasped. God does indeed grasp the reasons why the alcoholic refrains, since the alcoholic is acting against his disposition and in accord with an understanding of true goodness and happiness. God does not know the alcoholic's particular action of refusing the wine

tomorrow, since such particulars themselves are, in this strict sense, not subject to knowledge. But perhaps Gersonides' bold idea (although universally rejected by his contemporaries and successors) that humans exercise their God-given freedom *outside* divine providence, and even divine awareness, needs no explaining away.

Chapter 9
Society and the best life
(Ibn Ṭufayl and Dante)

Arguably, the fundamental question in ethics is simply: what is the best life, the one which makes a person happy, in the sense of flourishing as a human being? This question gives rise to a related, but more political one: what is the relation between an individual leading this best human life and human society? On the one side, to what extent is society required for an individual to live well? On the other side, does someone who is able to live the best life have a special part to play in society?

Ibn Ṭufayl, in early 12th-century Islamic Spain, and Dante, in Italy 200 years later, gave two of the most distinctive medieval answers to these questions. As will become clear, each of these authors developed their views in dialogue with a different strand of earlier writing and yet, although Dante certainly did not read Ibn Ṭufayl, the two are linked by an important thread of thinking which makes them both part of the same intellectual conversation. This thread is one already explored in Chapter 7: the idea of intellectual knowledge and the role in it of the Agent Intellect. In Arabic philosophy, this theme was given an ethical and political twist almost from the beginning. In the Latin World, the ethical dimension was quickly recognized, but it took a political form for the first time in Dante.

Although this conversation is an Aristotelian one, it rests on Platonic foundations: the political ideas developed by late

ancient thinkers such as Plotinus, Iamblichus, and Proclus, on the basis of Plato's *Republic* and *Laws*. More than three centuries before al-Fārābī, they had already been adapted by the Greek Christian thinker, pseudo-Dionysius (see Chapter 2). In his hierarchy of the Church, the bishops are made to play the part of Platonic guardians, and the ranks of initiators (priests and deacons) and initiated below them are arranged following the scheme of Platonic political thought. In (and beyond) the very final years of the Byzantine Empire, Gemistos Plethon (*c*.1360–1452), would return to this brand of political theory, de-Christianizing what his predecessor had so carefully put into the language of the Church.

Al-Fārābī and Ibn Bājja, Ibn Ṭufayl's predecessors

In the last book of his *Nicomachean Ethics*, Aristotle argues that the best life for humans, the one which brings happiness, is the life devoted to intellectual contemplation—that is, to using the intellect, thinking, and arguing, as philosophers do, about the unchanging patterns of things. Al-Fārābī wrote a commentary on the *Ethics* (now lost), and this idea of happiness influenced him deeply. He connected it to his account of the intellect (see Chapter 7). When the philosopher reaches a state of full knowledge, his intellect is conjoined with the Active Intellect, the lowest of the celestial intelligences. He also gives the theory a political twist, based on his reading of epitomes of Plato's *Republic* and *Laws*. There are many things, he observes, which humans cannot obtain individually. Life in society is necessary, both for bare subsistence and to live well. People live a good life, he argues, when they belong to a virtuous city, and a virtuous city is one with a ruler—al-Fārābī calls him indifferently a philosopher, prince, or imam—whose intellect has reached the state of conjunction with the Active Intellect. Such a ruler is the Aristotelian equivalent of the Guardians of Plato's ideal republic, who govern in accord with their knowledge of the Ideas.

The virtuous life lived by most citizens of a virtuous city would not, however, on al-Fārābī's account be the supremely happy one of intellectual contemplation, which only a few outstandingly able men can achieve. Most citizens lead good lives simply by playing their parts in the city's life, as determined by the ruler. They are unable to comprehend the scientific truths about the universe through their intellects, but they can be given an indirect understanding of them through metaphorical representations, as found in the world's different religions. Al-Fārābī believes that Islam gives a good metaphorical account, but of a truth which is fully grasped only by those capable of demonstration—an idea which he develops in his account of logic (see also Chapter 4). Given the level of most citizens' understanding, the ruler needs, as well as his intellectual gifts, the power to express truths in persuasive, imaginative form, and also the practical intelligence to engage in politics and bring his plans to reality.

Al-Fārābī considers that it is part of being a true philosopher to want to instruct others, within the limits of their capacities. Inspired by Plato, al-Fārābī treats the types of imperfect state in detail, but he does not think about how a virtuous person, who wishes to be a philosopher, should comport himself there (though he does believe that someone can be a philosopher, prince, and imam, even if no one obeys him). He pays much more attention to the people he describes as 'weeds'—those who live in a virtuous city but follow vicious inclinations.

In *The Conduct of the Solitary*, Ibn Bājja marks his difference from al-Fārābī by arguing that 'weeds' designates in general those whose opinions differ from those of their community, whether they are true opinions or not. In the perfectly virtuous city, the weeds would have, as al-Fārābī says, to be vicious—but then the city would not be perfectly virtuous. For Ibn Bājja, therefore, the weeds are those who dissent from their community by having true beliefs in a non-virtuous type of city.

He identifies these weeds with the 'solitary' of his title. But by 'solitary' (*mutawaḥḥid*) he means, not someone who literally isolates himself, but rather a person who is autonomous and preserves his own views and goals in the midst of those who think and act differently. Ibn Bājja accepts that life in a community is necessary, but he focuses on how someone can live well, even in a bad community (and he even holds out the hope that, because of these 'weeds', a perfect city will grow up; but he does not dwell on it).

Ibn Ṭufayl

The end to which the *mutawaḥḥid* strives is that of conjunction with the Active Intellect. In the preface to *Ḥayy ibn Yaqzān*, Ibn Ṭufayl criticizes Ibn Bājja for making a purely intellectual access to reality his goal, rather than the more tangible grasp, the 'taste', sought by those who follow a more spiritual, mystical path. As his choice of words makes clear, what he has in mind is Sufism: the ascetic, mystical form of Islam, of which he was an adept. None the less, Ibn Ṭufayl places himself in the tradition not only of al-Ghazālī, who had embraced Sufism along with *kalām* and, despite his criticisms of it, Avicennian philosophy, but also that of Avicenna himself, whose mystical side he (over)emphasizes.

What follows is not a treatise, but a philosophical tale. Ḥayy grows up, suckled by a deer, on an island otherwise without human inhabitants; either he was spontaneously generated there, or arrived, Moses-like, in a cradle entrusted to the mercy of the seas. The greater part of the story concerns his self-education. Ḥayy first learns about the world around him, discovering for himself what Ibn Ṭufayl's contemporaries would have recognized as scientific physics, biology, and cosmology. From this knowledge of the natural world, he progresses to an understanding of its creator—Avicenna's God, entirely one, necessary in itself and the cause of all else—and of his own immortal soul. This intellectual grasp of God makes Ḥayy desire, and eventually succeed in gaining

and being able to repeat and prolong at will, an immediate vision of God, in which his self is entirely lost.

Although Ḥayy is the only human being on his island, it would be wrong to conclude that his story so far has no ethical or political message. Aristotle's thinking about humans rests on the idea that they are social animals, who need to live in communities in order to flourish. Even the person given over to intellectual contemplation requires some support from other humans for the necessaries of life. Al-Fārābī, and even Ibn Bājja, followed this conception. Ibn Ṭufayl's thought experiment neatly rejects it, by showing that, in principle, someone can lead the very best possible life without having, or ever having had, any human society.

Ḥayy is not, however, depicted as living completely cut off from other things. Although in his mystic vision he abandons everything (himself included) except God, his path from philosophical knowledge to this state includes a long period where he lives in contact with all sorts of other animals and things, though not human beings, and takes an ethical attitude to them. He imitates the stars, in their motion and their purity; he helps animals which are hungry or wounded, and even plants from which the sun has been blocked; and he adopts a diet of fallen fruits so as to impede as little as possible their cycle of growth and reproduction. For Ibn Ṭufayl, as for Aristotle and al-Fārābī, the virtuous life which makes a person happy involves some other-directed behaviour, but the range of what is designated by 'other' is far wider for him than for them: not just fellow citizens or other humans, but the whole of the created universe, from the plants to the heavenly bodies.

Ḥayy does not remain in isolation. There is a neighbouring island where a religion has been introduced and become popular: one which goes back to 'one of the ancient prophets' and 'which expresses all true realities by likenesses which give images of them and imprint their traces in the mind'. Asal is a devotee of this

religion (which, of course, is in every respect like Islam, although Ibn Ṭufayl is careful not to identify it). He is always trying to penetrate beneath the literal meaning of its words and deepen his understanding, and he goes to Ḥayy's island to seek God in solitude. The two men meet and, when Ḥayy has been taught to speak and explains his knowledge of God and the universe, Asal immediately recognizes that all which his religion has taught are merely likenesses of the truth Ḥayy has grasped; and, on his side, Ḥayy accepts that this religion comes from God and has been preached by his prophet.

Ḥayy is amazed, however, when he hears from Asal about the worldliness of the islanders, despite their religion. He decides to go and teach them the truth openly, but he finds that, as soon he goes beyond the literal sense of their religion, they do not follow him. Ḥayy sees that he has made a mistake. He has not reckoned for their lack of intellectual ability and attachment to material things, and he tells them that they are right to stick to the literal sense of the religion and its practices, and not to try to search for deeper meanings. He and Asal return to their island, each to a life of solitary contemplation there.

Ḥayy's plan to teach the truth openly to ordinary people goes against the views of al-Fārābī. But it would be wrong to see Ibn Ṭufayl as implicitly criticizing Ḥayy for failing to do what, according to al-Fārābī, was required: to make himself a philosopher king, ruling in accord with his knowledge and presenting truths in the likenesses forged by his own imagination. The traditional religion, it is suggested, serves the inhabitants of Asal's island as well as any likeness of the truth could do. Moreover, the mystic, Sufi twist given to Ḥayy's goal makes it completely implausible that, like al-Fārābī's philosopher king, he would have knowledge relevant to ruling well, since the union he seeks with the divine involves a complete emptying of the mind. In so far as Ḥayy has relations with anything but God, they are with the wide world of living things and the cosmic hierarchy; the mass of people fit into it as

just one other sort of irrational animal, destined at death, it seems (despite some deliberate ambiguity), for extinction.

Augustine and Marsilius of Padua

In the *City of God*, Augustine breaks with ancient political thinking far more radically than any of the Arabic philosophers did, even ibn Ṭufayl. An initial aim of the work had been to attack the view of the Roman Empire, which grew up as it gradually became a Christian one, as God's empire on earth, divinely favoured with worldly power. But Augustine went further, rejecting the idea that any city in the world could approach the ideal of a community ruled by justice, as Plato's ideal republic, ruled by philosophers, was supposed to be.

Humanity is divided, Augustine thought, into two groups, which are not distinguished by any obvious outward sign: not by social status or intelligence or education, nor even by visible membership of the Christian community. Those destined for salvation belong to the City of God, but they must journey through life unknown to one another and mixed with the others, who belong to City of the World and are heading towards damnation. There is no happy life which it is possible to lead on earth, either for an individual, such as the ancients' philosopher sage, or for the inhabitants of a virtuous city. Augustine does, however, give a role to the political organization of society, but a more modest one. Rulers should aim at achieving peace, which is desired by all things and can be used by the members of the City of God on their pilgrimage to the heavenly bliss they will enjoy.

Although Augustine's works were never textbooks in the school or university curriculum, his influence on every aspect of thought in the Latin tradition was immense. In political philosophy, some medieval writers could not resist the temptation to identify the City of God with the Church. Augustine's real intentions were grasped by thinkers whose outlook seems, at first sight, to be very

distant from his. One of them was Marsilius of Padua (d. 1342). Marsilius was a Paris Arts Master who, like his friend, the Averroist, John of Jandun, took the imperial side in the conflict with the papacy and ended his life (together with John, William of Ockham, and other philosophers) in the entourage of the Emperor, Ludwig of Bavaria.

Much of his *Defender of the Peace* (1324) is devoted to attacking papal claims to secular political power, but the work also has a theoretical dimension. Following Aristotle's *Politics*—well-studied in the Latin universities but unavailable in the Islamic world—Marsilius sets out the different classes of people (farmers, soldiers, mechanics) needed to make up a city. He treats priests and their religious function in Aristotelian fashion. Their purpose is to serve the worldly good of the city. But Marsilius adds that the pagan views about God were mistaken, and he distinguishes earthly well-being from heavenly well-being, which he believes philosophy cannot treat.

Marsilius' procedure is comprehensible in the light of the sharp distinction that Arts Masters, beginning fifty years earlier with Siger of Brabant and Boethius of Dacia, often made between the sphere of knowledge open to reason and investigated by each of the disciplines set out by Aristotle's works according to their particular principles, and that of truths knowable only through revelation. Within Aristotelian political science, which is the rational way of thinking about human society, the purpose of religion is to promote the well-being of the city, and it does not matter whether or not religious claims are true, so long as they are generally believed. Just as, according to Boethius of Dacia, an Arts Master working in natural science must hold that the world has no beginning, even though, as a Christian, he knows that it did have one, so for Marsilius, the Arts Master treating politics should view religion in this Aristotelian way, despite the fact that he knows that Christianity alone is the true faith, which will lead to salvation.

There is a difference, though, because politics is a practical science. Marsilius wants cities to be organized according to his prescriptions, in which Christianity has a merely instrumental role. The result, he believes, will not be a Platonic sort of ideal city, but stability and peace. These are the best conditions for people to pursue their spiritual ends—ends which Marsilius acknowledges but which it is not his job to discuss. Though his starting point and the language could hardly be more different, Marsilius' ultimate political aims hardly differ from Augustine's.

Dante

Dante was an older contemporary of Marsilius who also, but in a more complex way, shows an underlying Augustinianism in his ideas about human happiness and society, although his starting point contrasts sharply with Augustine's. Many features of his *Monarchia* (1314) anticipate the *Defender of the Peace*. Dante too was a fierce of opponent of the papacy's claims to worldly power, and a supporter of the Imperial cause; one of his reasons for composing the treatise was probably to support Henry VII of Luxembourg's short-lived attempt to bring unity to Italy and revive the Empire.

Even more clearly than Marsilius, Dante gives a political form to the division of spheres between the arts and theology. There are two ends set by providence for humans, he asserts: happiness in this life, and the happiness of eternal life. Earthly happiness is reached through the teachings of philosophy, under the guidance of the Emperor; heavenly happiness through the revealed truth under the guidance of the Pope.

There are two important ways, however, in which Dante differs from Marsilius. The first is with regard to the size of political entity he discusses. Like most ancient and much medieval political thinking, the unit on which Marsilius concentrates is the city. Some writers in the Middle Ages thought, rather, about kingdoms,

but Dante is unique in considering that his polity—a revived, truly universal Roman Empire—should embrace all humankind. The second difference is in how he discusses the functioning of this polity. Marsilius takes his cue from Aristotle and looks at the different constituent classes and their roles. Dante is far more theoretical.

The starting point for Dante's theorizing is Aristotle's view of the best life as one of intellectual contemplation. Whereas, early in the Arabic philosophical tradition, al-Fārābī, with Platonic ideas about society in mind, gave this position a political twist, Arts Masters in the 13th-century universities thought of it as an aspiration for individuals—one, indeed, which only they, as philosophers, were in a position to attain.

Dante himself was not an Arts Master: already as a young man he was famed for his vernacular poetry, but he never went to university. He became interested in philosophy, however, through reading Cicero and Boethius, and he studied widely, assimilating and reworking ideas from Aquinas, Albert the Great, and the Arts Masters. His *Convivio*, written before the *Divine Comedy* and the *Monarchia*, belongs to a genre favoured by the Arts Masters: treatises on how dedication to philosophy leads to the happiest life. But the *Convivio* is an idiosyncratic example of the genre. Rather than hold, with the Arts Masters, that through philosophy we can even on earth fulfil our natural desire for the highest good, Dante believes that our natural desires are restricted to our capabilities. Philosophy does allow us, then, to fulfil these desires, but without bringing the knowledge of the highest good, God, which we hope to have in heaven.

In the *Monarchia*, Dante presents a social version of intellectual contemplation as the best life. What, he asks, is the goal of humanity *taken as a whole*? Taking, like Averroes, the possible intellect as one for all humans (a position he thought false, but could accept within the sphere of purely rational, philosophical

argument), he identifies this goal as actuating always the whole power of the possible intellect.

At first, it seems as if Dante wants all people to spend their time, so far as possible, in intellectual contemplation: a fine ideal, perhaps, but hardly a practicable or even a plausible one. But, as in the *Convivio*, it turns out that Dante has tempered the Arts Masters' triumphalist attitude to philosophy. He allows that there can be an 'extension' of the speculative intellect to the practical one. Humanity therefore can reach its goal through every sort of virtuous activity, not just by contemplation. The ideal of life for most of those in Dante's universal empire might not, then, be very different from that in al-Fārābī's perfect city, but whereas the people there are merely following the order set out by their philosopher king, Dante's world-citizens are engaged in a communal enterprise.

Despite his eulogistic attitude to the Roman Empire, Dante is still close to Augustine in his view of individual and social happiness. The goal Dante establishes for humanity demands the existence of a universal empire, because only through such government will there be the peace that will allow it to be reached. As in the *City of God*, then, peace is made the political goal, so as to open the possibility of a higher one. True, for Dante, by contrast with Augustine, the higher goal is two-fold: earthly life is no mere pilgrimage, and it can be fully understood and properly guided, in its own terms, through philosophical teaching. But the highest good, he would agree with Augustine, lies beyond this world, and it was to describing this ultimate goal for each human individually (and its opposite) that Dante dedicated his greatest work.

Chapter 10
Why medieval philosophy?

Why should anyone be bothered to learn about medieval philosophy? The question is an important one because in practice very few people *are* bothered to learn about it: very few, even, of those (such as professional philosophers) who would be ashamed if their ignorance extended to the philosophy of other periods. And it might seem that here, at the end of this book, there is an easy way to answer the question. Since it is now clear that there was a great deal of excellent philosophy written in the Middle Ages, is there not as much reason to learn about it as to learn about excellent philosophy from any other period?

But there is an obvious objection to this answer. Most philosophers justify learning about philosophy from the past principally by the contribution it can make to present-day philosophizing, either by providing arguments or positions that can still be adopted, or at least by contributing more broadly to the contemporary debate. Medieval philosophy is far less suited to this role than the philosophy of other periods because its concepts and assumptions (especially the scientific theories it uses) are much more distant from ours than those of more recent thinkers, and because of its links with revealed religion, which are much closer than for philosophy today or indeed for ancient Greek philosophy. Moreover, even if, with enough historical work, contemporary philosophers were able to find valuable material for their own work in medieval

sources, why should they make such efforts, when philosophy from other periods offers its fruits so much more easily?

On its own terms, this objection is indisputable. But it can and should be rejected by challenging two fundamental assumptions on which it is based. The first assumption is about *why* philosophers should learn about philosophy from the past. The second is about *who* should be interested in the history of philosophy.

If the value of past philosophy really lay in the direct contribution it can make to contemporary discussions, then it would not be worth taking the trouble to learn about *any* past period of philosophy. Only very rarely is a new argument that is important for current debate discovered in an old text, and it could probably have been reached with far less effort by thinking about the contemporary problem. This is not to say that the philosophical explorations of the past have not contributed to how topics are discussed today, but their contributions have been adapted, absorbed, and integrated into the standard presentation of the problems.

The real contribution the history of philosophy can make to contemporary philosophy is indirect. Since philosophy is a practice that has grown up among the contingencies of history, learning about its past and its changing relationship to other practices and the wider human predicament is the only way to understand more about what sort of practice it is; and that question is one which is intrinsic to philosophy.

Philosophers, however, are not the only people who should be interested in the history of philosophy. An outline knowledge, at least, of the history of philosophy is part of the equipment any man or woman needs for understanding the world, not so much because of the claims philosophers now make (which are usually limited), but because of those they have made in the past.

There are, then, besides the specialists in the history of philosophy themselves, two constituencies for the history of philosophy: philosophers trying to understand the nature of their own practice, and non-philosophers seeking an essential element in their understanding of the world and its past. For both purposes, learning about the history of philosophy must not be an exercise in pillaging the past of its treasures, but one in understanding honestly, so far as we can, how people really once thought, and how they did so through time. To omit, or drastically to distort, any significant period in the history of philosophy is, therefore, damaging to both constituencies. But to omit medieval philosophy is more than just the omission of a significant period, it is the omission of most of Western philosophy—1,500 years out of a period of about 2,500—and of the period when, more than in any other, philosophy was at the centre of intellectual life and cultivated by the most brilliant minds.

When they omit or marginalize the Middle Ages, historians of philosophy do not tell an honest story. The standard university history of philosophy course, which jumps as if over an abyss from Aristotle to Descartes, or many a standard textbook history, with its meagre and narrowly focused chapter on the Middle Ages, is more likely to inculcate ignorance than knowledge about how philosophy has developed and its role in human history.

There are two misconceptions, in particular, about Western philosophy and its history that even a slight acquaintance with medieval philosophy will dispel. First, the history that is told of Western philosophy is usually Eurocentric (extended to other Anglophone countries for the last century and a half) and culturally monolithic, in that it normally excludes not just those who lived outside the borders of Europe, but also the Jews who lived inside them, except for those who abandoned their Jewish faith. Investigating medieval thought with an open mind, tracing its various developments and how they have interrelated, shows that Western philosophy is a unified tradition, but not a

monolithic one: it is culturally and religiously diverse, involving paganism, Judaism, Islam, and Christianity in all its forms; as fluent in Semitic languages as Indo-European ones; no less at home in the steppes of Central Asia than by the banks of the Seine or the Isis.

Second, although Muslims and Jews have been particularly scorned by historians of Western philosophy, Christianity has not been much favoured either. With some exceptions, they have tried to leave religion out of their account of philosophy, or have represented it as an antagonist. In all four traditions, medieval philosophy is deeply implicated in religious problems and practices, and although there was certainly, at times, antagonism, the relations between philosophical reasoning and revealed faiths were clearly far too complex to be captured by this or by any single formula. Medieval philosophy shows that the history of philosophy cannot be understood apart from the history of religions, not just because this is true for the millennium and a half over which it stretches, but because it points to how philosophy and religion were intertwined before then, and for long afterwards.

Timeline

Philosophers (date of death unless otherwise indicated)	Events and institutions
270 Plotinus	
c.305 Porphyry	
	306–37 Reign of Constantine, first Christian Roman Emperor
430 Augustine	410 Sack of Rome by Alaric
485 Proclus	476 Romulus Augustulus, last Western Roman Emperor, deposed
c.525 Boethius; 536 Sergius of Reshʻaina	529 School of Athens closed by Justinian
570s John Philoponus	
	632 Death of the Prophet Muḥammad
	641 Fall of Alexandria to Muslims
662 Maximus the Confessor	661 Beginning of Umayyad Caliphate
Before 754 John of Damascus	749 Beginning of ʻAbbāsid Caliphate; 762 Construction of capital at Baghdad commissioned
806 Alcuin	800 Charlemagne crowned as Emperor

c.870 John Scottus Eriugena; after 870 al-Kindī; 891 Photius; c.907 Isaac Israeli	843–77 Reign of Charles the Bald; 843 End of iconoclasm in Byzantium
935-6 al-Ashʿarī; 942 Saadia Gaon; 950/1 al-Fārābī	
1037 Avicenna; 1057/58 Ibn Gabirol	973 Cairo established as Fāṭimid capital
1085 al-Juwaynī; 1096 Michael Psellos; 1109 Anselm of Canterbury; 1111 al-Ghazāli	1085 Toledo falls to the Christians; 1090 Almoravid rule in Spain begins
1139 Ibn Bājja; 1142 Peter Abelard; 1154 Gilbert of Poitiers	1147 Almohads defeat Almoravids
1160 al-Baghdādī; 1185 Ibn Ṭufayl	c.1200 Establishment of University of Paris
1191 Suhrawardī; 1198 Averroes; 1204 Fakhr al-Dīn al-Razī	1204 Constantinople sacked and Latin Kingdom established there
	c.1210 Establishment of Franciscan and Dominican Orders
1240 Ibn ʿArabi; 1245 Alexander of Hales	c.1255 Aristotelian curriculum adopted in Arts Faculties of Paris and Oxford
	1258 Mongols take Baghdad; 1259 Establishment of Marāgha observatory
1274 Thomas Aquinas; Bonaventure; al-Ṭūsī; 1276 al-Kātibī; 1280 Albert the Great	1277 Tempier's condemnation of 219 Propositions at Paris
1293 Henry of Ghent; 1298 Peter John Olivi; 1308 Duns Scotus	
1315 Ramon Llull; 1318/20 Dietrich of Freiberg; 1321 Dante Alighieri;	1323 Canonization of Thomas Aquinas
1327/8 Meister Eckhart; 1328 Ibn Taymiyya	

1342 Marsilius of Padua; 1344 Gersonides; 1347 William of Ockham; 1355 al-Ījī	c.1346–53 Black Death
1359 Gregory Palamas; 1360 John Buridan; after 1362 Moses of Narbonne	
1384 John Wyclif	
1410/11 Ḥasdai Crescas	1415 Execution of Jan Hus, leading to Hussite rebellion
1429 Paul of Venice; 1444 John Capreolus; 1454 Gemisthos Plethon	
1457 Lorenzo Valla; 1460 Heymeric of Campo; 1464 Nicholas of Cusa	c.1450 Moveable printing type introduced in Europe; 1453 Fall of Constantinople to Turks
1493 Elijah Delmedigo; 1498 Ṣadr al-Dīn Dashtakī; 1494 Giovanni Pico della Mirandola	1492 Columbus's first voyage; 1492 Expulsion of Jews and Muslims from Spain
1499 Marsilio Ficino; 1501 al-Dawānī; 1508 Isaac Abrabanel	
After 1521 Leone Ebreo; 1525 Pietro Pomponazzi; 1538 Agostino Nifo	1521 Excommunication of Martin Luther
1546 Francisco de Vitoria; 1550 John Major	1545–63 Council of Trent
1589 Jacopo Zabarella	1598 Edict of Nantes
1617 Francisco Suárez	
1630 Mir Dāmād; 1636 Mulla Ṣadrā;	1633 Condemnation of Galileo
1644 John of St Thomas; 1650 René Descartes	1642–51 English Civil War
1667 Rodrigo de Arriaga; 1677 Baruch Spinoza; 1682 Juan Caramuel y Lobkowitz	1685 Revocation of Edict of Nantes
1704 John Locke; 1716 G. W. Leibniz	

References

These notes aim merely to note the sources for the main parts of the discussions in Chapters 6–9, and to give details of English translations, where they have been made.

Chapter 6: Universals (Avicenna and Abelard)

Avicenna, see his *Cure* V.1–2, translated (with parallel text), Michael E. Marmura as *The Metaphysics of* The Healing (Provo, Utah, 2005). See also the extract from the *Cure* commentary on the *Isagoge*, as translated in Michael E. Marmura, 'Avicenna's Chapter on Universals in the *Isagoge* of his *Shifā''* in *Islam: Past Influence and Present Challenge*, ed. Alford T. Welch and Pierre Cachia (Edinburgh, 1979), pp. 47–52. See also Alain de Libera, *L'art des généralités: Théories de l'abstraction* (Paris, 1999) for a good French translation of the central text and a thorough analysis.

Boethius (second commentary on *Isagoge*), Abelard (*Logica Ingredientibus, Isagoge* commentary), Scotus (*Ordinatio* II, d. 3, part 1, qq. 1–6), and Ockham (*Ordinatio* I, d. 2, qq. 4–8), see the translations in Paul V. Spade, *Five Texts on the Mediaeval Problem of Universals* (Indianapolis, Indiana, and Cambridge, 1994).

Chapter 7: Mind, body, and mortality (Averroes and Pomponazzi)

Al-Fārābī, *The Principles of the Views of the Citizens of the Best City* (especially Chapter 3), translated Richard Walzer as *Al-Farabi on the Perfect State* (Oxford, 1985).

For a short presentation of Avicenna's views, see the extract from *al-Najat* in *Medieval Islamic Philosophical Writings*, ed. Muhammad A. Khalidi (Cambridge, 2005), pp. 27–58.

Averroes, *Long Commentary on the* De anima *of Aristotle*, translated and introduced Richard C. Taylor (New Haven and London, 2009).

Aquinas, see especially his *On the Unity of the Intellect*, translated by Ralph McInerny as *Aquinas Against the Averroists: On There Being Only One Intellect* (West Lafayette, Indiana, 1993) and *Summa theologiae* I, q. 76 (there are various translations, including one available freely on the web).

Pomponazzi, the translation of *On the Immortality of the Soul* in *The Renaissance Philosophy of Man*, ed. Ernst Cassirer, Paul O. Kristeller, and John H. Randall, Jr (Chicago and London, 1948), pp. 280–381.

Chapter 8: Foreknowledge and freedom (Boethius and Gersonides)

Boethius, *Consolation of Philosophy*, Book V. There are many translations. That by Joel Relihan (Indianapolis and Cambridge, 2001) is especially close. For a fuller exposition of this interpretation, see John Marenbon, 'Divine Prescience and Contingency in Boethius's *Consolation of Philosophy*', *Rivista di storia della filosofia* 68 (2013), 9–21.

Abelard and early 13th-century writers: for texts and discussion, see John Marenbon, *Le temps, l'éternité et la prescience de Boèce à Thomas d'Aquin* (Paris, 2005), pp. 55–116.

Duns Scotus, *Lectura* on *Sentences* I, d. 39, published, with translation and commentary by A. Vos Jaczn et al. as *John Duns Scotus. Contingency and Freedom: Lectura I 39* (Dordrecht, Boston, and London, 1994) (New Synthese Historical Library 42).

Avicenna, *Metaphysics* VI.6 (trans. Marmura, chapter 5, pp. 287–90).

Averroes, *Metaphysics* Book Lam, translated by Charles Gennequand as *Ibn Rushd's Metaphysics* (Leiden, 1984) (Islamic Philosophy and Theology: Texts and Studies, 1), pp. 197–8.

Maimonides, *Guide of the Perplexed* III.20–1, translated Shlomo Pines (Chicago, 1963).

Gersonides, *Wars of the Lord*, III.3–4 and, for theory of providence, II.4, Seymour Feldman (Philadelphia, Jewish Theological

Seminary of America, vol. II, 1997. See also especially Charles H. Manekin, 'On the Limited-Omniscience Interpretation of Gersonides' Theory of Divine Knowledge' in *Perspective on Jewish Thought and Mysticism*, ed. Alfred L. Ivry, Elliot R. Wolfson, and Allan Arkush (Amsterdam, Harwood (OPA), 1998), pp. 135–70.

Chapter 9: Society and the best life (Ibn Ṭufayl and Dante)

Late ancient and Byzantine Platonic political philosophy: see Dominic J. O'Meara, *Platonic Political Philosophy in Late Antiquity* (Oxford, 2003).

Al-Fārābī, *Principles of the Views* (see under Chapter 7).

Ibn Bājja, *The Life of the Solitary*. No English translation, but there is an edition of the text with a parallel translation into French: *La conduit de l'isolé et deux autres épîtres*, ed. Charles Gennequand (Paris, 2010).

Ibn Ṭufayl, *Hayy ibn Yaqzān*, trans. Lenn Goodman (New York, 1972).

Augustine, *City of God*, trans. Henry Bettenson (Harmondsworth, 1972).

Marsilius of Padua, *Defender of the Peace*, trans. Annabel Brett (Cambridge, 2005).

Dante, *Monarchia*, trans. Prue Shaw (Cambridge, 1996).

Further reading

Encyclopaedic resources

The best place for discussions of individual authors and themes in medieval philosophy is the *Stanford Encylopedia of Philosophy*, freely available online at <http://plato.stanford.edu/>. The coverage is still far from complete, but it is being increased all the time, and the articles are usually full discussions, written by experts. Some entries, indeed (such as that on Arabic logic), are the places to find the very latest research. The *Encyclopaedia of Medieval Philosophy*, ed. Henrik Lagerlund (Dordrecht, Heidelberg, London, and New York, 2011—and available online, paying, from Springer) goes up to 1500 and is more complete. The entries vary in their level, but the treatment of Arabic philosophy is usually especially good. I have contributed a long bibliography on medieval philosophy to Oxford Bibliographies (online, paying: <http://www.oxfordbibliographies.com/>).

General introductions, handbooks, and histories

Few books which claim to introduce or to tell the history of medieval philosophy cover anything like the full range of the subject. My *Medieval Philosophy: An Historical and Philosophical Introduction* (London and New York, 2007)—not to be confused with my earlier *Introductions* to *Earlier* and *Later Medieval Philosophy*, published in the 1980s—does at least cover the four main traditions and provides an obvious sequel to the present, short book (with full bibliography). Unfortunately, it stops, abruptly, at 1400. *The Cambridge History of Medieval Philosophy*, ed. Robert Pasnau (Cambridge, 2014, revised edition) avowedly covers Islamic, Jewish, and Christian material

(up to about 1500), but most of the (topic-based) chapters are predominantly on the Latin Christian tradition, and especially the period 1250–1350, although it adds very valuable lists of translations from Greek into Latin and Arabic, and Arabic into Latin and bio-bibliographical notices covering all the traditions. *The Oxford Handbook of Medieval Philosophy* (New York, 2012), which I edited, suffers even more badly from the same narrowness in its topic-based chapters, but the first 250 pages provide a summary history, written by experts, of the four traditions, up to the 17th century. *The Cambridge Companion to Medieval Philosophy*, ed. Stephen McGrade (Cambridge, 2003), which contains mostly topic-based, exploratory essays, gives just two chapters out of fourteen to Islamic and Jewish philosophy. Anthony Kenny's volume on medieval philosophy, in his *New History of Western Philosophy* (Oxford, 2005), displays all its author's characteristic learning, clarity, and acuity, but treats Arabic and Jewish philosophy only in so far as they influenced the Latin tradition.

Introductions, handbooks, and histories of individual traditions or periods

In order, therefore, to gain a rounded introduction to the area, readers must supplement these general books with volumes devoted to particular traditions or periods. There is nothing satisfactory on Byzantine philosophy. On Arabic philosophy, *The Cambridge Companion to Arabic Philosophy*, ed. Peter Adamson and Richard Taylor (Cambridge, 2005) provides a good survey, with stimulating, and often quite demanding chapters, though there is not much on *kalām* nor on the period from 1100 to 1500. *The History of Islamic Philosophy*, ed. Seyyed Nasr and Oliver Leaman (London and New York, 1996) (Routledge History of World Philosophies 1) has a wide coverage, but veers in its interests towards illuminationism and mysticism. On Jewish philosophy, there are the thoughtful, author-based essays which make up *The Cambridge Companion to Medieval Jewish Philosophy*, ed. Daniel Frank and Oliver Leaman (Cambridge, 2003) and *The Cambridge History of Jewish Philosophy from Antiquity through the Seventeenth Century*, ed. Steven Nadler and Tamara Rudavsky (Cambridge, 2009), with topically organized chapters, which sensibly includes Spinoza within its time span.

On the period from 1400 to 1600 in the Latin tradition, there are a variety of general works on so-called Renaissance philosophy. *The Cambridge History of Renaissance Philosophy*, ed. Charles Schmitt and Quentin Skinner (Cambridge, 1988) is arranged by areas of philosophy and, though now a little dated, remains fundamental. *The Cambridge Companion to Renaissance Philosophy*, ed. James Hankins (Cambridge, 2007), brings out the variety of thinking in this period, and *Renaissance Philosophy*, ed. Brian Copenhaver and Charles Schmitt (Oxford and New York, 1992), is perhaps the best, rounded introduction to the period.

It is all but impossible to find a guide to 17th-century philosophy which gives the continuity with the earlier tradition due weight: for an initial orientation, read Jacob Schmutz's chapter on 'Medieval Philosophy after the Middle Ages' in *The Oxford Handbook of Medieval Philosophy*. Finally, Richard Cross's *The Medieval Christian Philosophers: An Introduction* is explicitly limited to the Christian (Latin) tradition, and looks only at the period from *c*.1100 to 1350, concentrating on its final century. Although this is the most well-trodden ground in the whole area, its penetrating presentation of the very important thinkers it covers, especially Scotus and Ockham, make it very valuable, and a good antidote to the view of the field I have tried to offer.

Index

Figures from the Latin and Greek traditions born before 1500 are normally listed under the Christian name (e.g. Aquinas is under Thomas Aquinas). Writers in Arabic and Hebrew are listed under the names usually used.

Index

PHILOSOPHY IN THE ISLAMIC WORLD
A Very Short Introduction
Peter Adamson

In the history of philosophy, few topics are so relevant to today's cultural and political landscape as philosophy in the Islamic world. Yet, this remains one of the lesser-known philosophical traditions. In this *Very Short Introduction*, Peter Adamson explores the history of philosophy among Muslims, Jews, and Christians living in Islamic lands.

Introducing the main philosophical themes of the Islamic world, Adamson integrates ideas from the Islamic and Abrahamic faiths to consider the broad philosophical questions that continue to invite debate. Drawing on the most recent research in the field, this book challenges the assumption of the cultural decline of philosophy and science in the Islamic world by demonstrating its rich heritage and overlap with other faiths and philosophies.

www.oup.com/vsi

ECONOMICS
A Very Short Introduction
Partha Dasgupta

Economics has the capacity to offer us deep insights into some of the most formidable problems of life, and offer solutions to them too. Combining a global approach with examples from everyday life, Partha Dasgupta describes the lives of two children who live very different lives in different parts of the world: in the Mid-West USA and in Ethiopia. He compares the obstacles facing them, and the processes that shape their lives, their families, and their futures. He shows how economics uncovers these processes, finds explanations for them, and how it forms policies and solutions.

'An excellent introduction ... presents mathematical and statistical findings in straightforward prose.'

Financial Times

www.oup.com/vsi

THE EUROPEAN UNION
A Very Short Introduction
John Pinder & Simon Usherwood

This *Very Short Introduction* explains the European Union in plain English. Fully updated for 2007 to include controversial and current topics such as the Euro currency, the EU's enlargement, and its role in ongoing world affairs, this accessible guide shows how and why the EU has developed from 1950 to the present. Covering a range of topics from the Union's early history and the ongoing interplay between 'eurosceptics' and federalists, to the single market, agriculture, and the environment, the authors examine the successes and failures of the EU, and explain the choices that lie ahead in the 21st century.

www.oup.com/vsi

GEOGRAPHY
A Very Short Introduction
John A. Matthews & David T. Herbert

Modern Geography has come a long way from its historical
roots in exploring foreign lands, and simply mapping and naming
the regions of the world. Spanning both physical and human
Geography, the discipline today is unique as a subject which
can bridge the divide between the sciences and the
humanities, and between the environment and our society.
Using wide-ranging examples from global warming and oil,
to urbanization and ethnicity, this *Very Short Introduction* paints
a broad picture of the current state of Geography, its subject
matter, concepts and methods, and its strengths and
controversies. The book's conclusion is no less than
a manifesto for Geography' future.

'Matthews and Herbert's book is written- as befits the VSI series- in
an accessible prose style and is peppered with attractive and
understandable images, graphs and tables.'

Geographical.

GLOBAL WARMING
A Very Short Introduction
Mark Maslin

Global warming is arguably the most critical and controversial issue facing the world in the twenty-first century. This *Very Short Introduction* provides a concise and accessible explanation of the key topics in the debate: looking at the predicted impact of climate change, exploring the political controversies of recent years, and explaining the proposed solutions. Fully updated for 2008, Mark Maslin's compelling account brings the reader right up to date, describing recent developments from US policy to the UK Climate Change Bill, and where we now stand with the Kyoto Protocol. He also includes a chapter on local solutions, reflecting the now widely held view that, to mitigate any impending disaster, governments as well as individuals must to act together.

www.oup.com/vsi

GLOBALIZATION
A Very Short Introduction
Manfred Steger

'Globalization' has become one of the defining buzzwords of our time - a term that describes a variety of accelerating economic, political, cultural, ideological, and environmental processes that are rapidly altering our experience of the world. It is by its nature a dynamic topic - and this *Very Short Introduction* has been fully updated for 2009, to include developments in global politics, the impact of terrorism, and environmental issues. Presenting globalization in accessible language as a multifaceted process encompassing global, regional, and local aspects of social life, Manfred B. Steger looks at its causes and effects, examines whether it is a new phenomenon, and explores the question of whether, ultimately, globalization is a good or a bad thing.

www.oup.com/vsi

NUCLEAR POWER
A Very Short Introduction
Maxwell Irvine

The term 'nuclear power' causes anxiety in many people and there is confusion concerning the nature and extent of the associated risks. Here, Maxwell Irvine presents a concise introduction to the development of nuclear physics leading up to the emergence of the nuclear power industry. He discusses the nature of nuclear energy and deals with various aspects of public concern, considering the risks of nuclear safety, the cost of its development, and waste disposal. Dispelling some of the widespread confusion about nuclear energy, Irvine considers the relevance of nuclear power, the potential of nuclear fusion, and encourages informed debate about its potential.

www.oup.com/vsi

DESERTS
A Very Short Introduction
Nick Middleton

Deserts make up a third of the planet's land surface, but if you picture a desert, what comes to mind? A wasteland? A drought? A place devoid of all life forms? Deserts are remarkable places. Typified by drought and extremes of temperature, they can be harsh and hostile; but many deserts are also spectacularly beautiful, and on occasion teem with life. Nick Middleton explores how each desert is unique: through fantastic life forms, extraordinary scenery, and ingenious human adaptations. He demonstrates a desert's immense natural beauty, its rich biodiversity, and uncovers a long history of successful human occupation. This *Very Short Introduction* tells you everything you ever wanted to know about these extraordinary places and captures their importance in the working of our planet.

www.oup.com/vsi

AMERICAN POLITICAL PARTIES AND ELECTIONS
A Very Short Introduction
Sandy L. Maisel

Few Americans and even fewer citizens of other nations understand the electoral process in the United States. Still fewer understand the role played by political parties in the electoral process or the ironies within the system. Participation in elections in the United States is much lower than in the vast majority of mature democracies. Perhaps this is because of the lack of competition in a country where only two parties have a true chance of winning, despite the fact that a large number of citizens claim allegiance to neither and think badly of both. Studying these factors, you begin to get a very clear picture indeed of the problems that underlay this much trumpeted electoral system.

www.oup.com/vsi

ONLINE
CATALOGUE
A Very Short Introduction

Our online catalogue is designed to make it easy to find your ideal Very Short Introduction. View the entire collection by subject area, watch author videos, read sample chapters, and download reading guides.

http://fds.oup.com/www.oup.co.uk/general/vsi/index.html

SOCIAL MEDIA
Very Short Introduction

Join our community
www.oup.com/vsi

- Join us online at the official Very Short Introductions **Facebook** page.
- Access the thoughts and musings of our authors with our online **blog**.
- Sign up for our monthly **e-newsletter** to receive information on all new titles publishing that month.
- Browse the full range of Very Short Introductions online.
- Read **extracts** from the Introductions for free.
- Visit our library of **Reading Guides**. These guides, written by our expert authors will help you to question again, why you think what you think.
- If you are a teacher or lecturer you can order inspection copies quickly and simply via our website.